T4-AKG-291

A Voice from the Byzantine East

Archbishop Elias Zoghby

Melkite Greek Catholic
Eparch of Baalbeck, Lebanon (*retired*)

Translated by R. Bernard

Educational Services
Diocese of Newton
West Newton, MA 02165

Archbishop Elias Zoghby served the Melkite Church as Patriarchal Vicar : Egypt and the Sudan from 1954-1968 and as Eparch of Baalback, Leban from 1968 until his retirement in 1987. He is the author of *Reflections a Proverbs* (in Arabic) and *Quand l'Eveque cancane, Tous Schismatiques?* a *St Matthieu lu par un Eveque d'Orient* (all in French). An English translati of *Tous Schismatiques?* is awaiting publication.

Cover design by Beverly Stoller, Studio of the Theotokos.

Library of Congress Cataloging-in-Publication Data

Zoghby, Elias.
    [Essays. English. Selections]
    A Voice from the Byzantine East / Elias Zoghby; translated by R. Bernard.
    p. cm.
    Translation of articles originally published in Le Lien, 1963-1970.
    ISBN 1-56125-018-X
    1. Catholic Church - Byzantine rite, Melchite - Relations - Orthod Eastern Church. 2. Orthodox Eastern Church - Relations - Catholic Churc Byzantine rite, Melchite. 3. Christian Union - Catholic Church. 4. Christian Union - Orthodox Eastern Church. 5. Catholic Church - Byzantine rite - Doctrines. 6. Popes - Primacy. I. Title.
BX4711.34.Z64 1992
281' .5 - dc20   92-13838
                                                                        CIP

Published by Educational Services, Diocese of Newton, 19 Dartmouth Stre West Newton, MA 02165.
Printed in the United States of America.

Table of Contents

Introduction

In his book *The Catholic Moment*, Richard John Neuhaus
ıt forth the thesis that the state of religion in the '80s was such that
was the right time for the Roman Catholic Church to make a
ajor contribution to the faith of all Christians. The late '50s were
ıch a moment for the Melkite community. After almost 100 years
 an unchecked increase in Roman centralization, the Melkite
ıiscopate under the leadership of Patriarch Maximos IV
·earheaded a movement to curtail this direction, which culminated
 the convocation of the Second Vatican Council.

A notable figure in the Melkite hierarchy at that time was
rchbishop Elias Zoghby, recently retired as Eparch of Baalbeck,
ebanon. At that time Archbishop of Nubia and patriarchal vicar
·r the Melkites in Egypt and the Sudan, he made eleven addresses
· "interventions" at Vatican II on many of the topics treated in
ese essays, which for the most part originally appeared in *Le Lien*,
urnal of the Melkite patriarchate. Archbishop Zoghby became
idely known among the bishops and theologians present at the
ouncil as well as to the press as a spokesman for reform.

In his introduction to the 1970 French edition of this work,
om Olivier Rousseau described Archbishop Elias as "the *enfant*
rible of the Melkite Catholic episcopate" (he was 52 years old at
e beginning of the Council). Perhaps it would be more appropriate
 think of him as a prophet and forerunner, a number of whose
·eas have since been either realized or more widely circulated. One
inks particularly of the current statements on Uniatism of the
rthodox - Roman Catholic Dialogue which echoes the thoughts of
rchbishop Elias in chapters nine, ten and eleven, written twenty
·ars before.

Other ideas are as jarring now as they were twenty years
;o. Thus he suggests boldly that God has worked through the
hism to preserve Orthodoxy from excessive centralization, that we
astern Catholics *are* Uniates, at home neither in Orthodoxy nor
oman Catholicism and that our principal ecumenical witness
ould be to point out to the true partners in the East-West
alogue our experience both as Eastern Christians and as Uniates.

It will be left for history to decide whether Archbishop Zoghby h been a "voice crying in the wilderness" on these questions.

For this present edition we have rearranged the chapte under new principal headings and, in addition to translator's not [R.B.], appended a number of end notes by this editor [F.S designed to note any changes in discipline or circumstances sin the original writing.

We are all indebted to Archbishop Ignatius Ghattas, Epar of Newton, for his encouragement and to the Chicagoland Melki community, under the patronage of St. John the Baptist, for maki possible the publication of these essays by a prophet and forerunn of our own time whose words the Church still needs to hear.

Rev. Fred Saato
Director of Educational Services

Part I - One and Catholic

The life of the Church is nothing less than the large scale production of the life of each individual soul. In its two thousand ars of existence, the Christian Church has undergone the same igious experience as the individual Christian, facing the same ses and the same conflicts as he does.

God, perfectly One in the Trinity, in creating a world of ments so varied and sometimes even opposed, intended to make nifest His glory and power by placing and maintaining unity in s world. Having created heaven and earth, animals and vegeta- n, the day star and the stars of the night, He gathered them all gether in amazingly beautiful harmony and in flawless order. merging from the eternal mind of God, this unity is both the pat- n and the foundation of all that is good and genuinely beautiful.[1]

But the material unity of the universe - which is comprised the harmony between the elements composing it and in the lance of their relations with each other - this Beautiful unity of ich God alone is the Author, is destined in His divine plan to epare the way for and stimulate that other unity which every man called upon to achieve within himself and also in the great human mily to which he belongs.

Within himself, unity consists of the harmony of all relations man's soul and body, spirit and senses. It is the coordination of all s activities, both spiritual and material, into a unified effort and wards a single goal.

Unity within oneself[2] cannot but help in achieving unity for man society. To accomplish this requires a conscious awareness all peoples of their common origins and destiny. This leads to eir interdependence, and to their dependence upon Him Who ade them all. Could we say that men have failed in realizing this uble unity?

Apart from a few exceptions, man is divided even within mself. The senses, dominated by their own pleasures, reduce the irit to slavery. The soul, made captive by the body, finds itself a isoner of its own instincts. Concupiscence of the flesh, concupis- nce of the eyes and the pride of life, if not combatted, will shatter e unity of the human being and install two men within one person.

"My own actions bewilder me; What I do is not what I wish but something which I hate." (Romans 7:1)3.

Divided within himself, threatened with the ruin of hi being, contemporary man is cast in the impossible role of u himself to his brothers. Nothing can be constructed on ruins su these; Order cannot be built on disorder. One cannot unite without those who are divided from within: "What leads to war, leads to quarreling among you? I will tell you what leads to the appetites which infest your mortal bodies!" (James 4:1).

Division in a family, division in a nation, division a peoples must be overcome. It seems that the links of the flesl blood of the sons of Adam have not been strong enough to man to his own kind any more than union of soul and body human being has been able to bring about the unity of man v himself. God's plan seems to have failed. Human nature appe be in need of restoration, rebirth, or even recreation. It needs a society, a supernatural one that is above race, and which can about, on a transcendental plane, the unity of its members.

We often overlook the most important event in huma tory. We forget that God gave us a new Adam, Jesus Christ, a Him, a new man, a new society: the Church - the assembly c children of God from every nation, race and human conc Henceforth, the Christian is born to a new life in Baptism. H say with Saint Paul: "It is no longer I who live, but Christ whc in me." In the Christian as in Saint Paul, there can no longer b men but one, Jesus Christ! There are not two wills, one prop good, the other advocating evil; there is but a single will; tl God. Living in Christ Jesus, the Christian must benefit fror balance reigning in the faculties of mind and senses of the S God, united in one thought and in one love.4

The Church, the assembly of the faithful participating same divine life and receiving the same Bread, must hence identify herself with Jesus and, with Him, constitute one single tical Body of which He is the head and we the members. Nc must be permitted to break the unity of the Body, for nothing separate the Christian from his Savior: "Nothing therefore can between us and the love of Christ, even if we are troubled or ried, or being persecuted, or lacking food or clothes, or threatened or even attacked." (Romans 8: 35; also see vs. 36-39

But where do we stand on this today? Where doe Christian faith itself stand? Where is our Christian solidarity ir

evil and atheistic materialism? In our confusion we cry out: "Let
 unite to cast out the evil that pervades the world!" However, this
 wasted effort, for it is only after fighting the evil within ourselves
 at we can unite against the evil threatening the world. Unity
nong Christians depends on union of each Christian with Christ.
'e cannot attain Christian unity if we are not continuously being
born in Christ Jesus, or if we are not living in and through Him.
'e must "cast off the old self whose way of life [we] well remember,
e self that wasted its aim on false dreams ... [and] be clothed in
ew self which is created in God's image, justified and sanctified
rough the truth," as Saint Paul reminds both us and the Ephesians
Eph. 5: 22-24). Whoever ceases being one with Christ ceases being
ne with himself, and at the same time, ceases being one with his
others and, consequently, one with the Church.

In brief, then, if Christianity is disunited we must look for
e cause of this disunion within the human passions, the three con-
upiscences, and in our own sins.

Individual sanctification and Christian unity go hand in
and. They are intertwined in the plan of salvation. The Son of God
ame to free us from sin and join us to Himself. To the extent that
is incorporation in Christ is achieved, to the extent we grow up,
rowing and incorporating ourselves into Christ" (Eph. 4: 15), to
at same extent will the Church, which is the Body of Christ, grow
to its own fullness.

This explains why Our Lord, when on the threshold of
mbracing His redemptive passion, seemed to forget why He had
iffered and preached, and seemed to make Christian unity instead,
e sole object of His suffering and of His prayer, especially of His
rayer in the garden: "that all may be one." During His public life,
e had recommended that His followers imitate God in all things,
eeking to be perfect as the Father is perfect *par excellence*. It is
pparent that up to the very moment when He prepared to seal His
iving mission with the mark of His blood, His human nature still
ees in God one remarkable thing to imitate, His unity.

Redemption and Christian unity are, therefore, intertwined
n the Divine Plan. The success of the first is determined by the suc-
ess of the other. Since our desire for Christian unity is contingent
pon our adherence to the redeeming Christ, it is essential for us to
now just how strongly we really desire unity. Do we sincerely want
nity, or are we indifferent to it? The reply to this query will be the
nswer, too, to the question of whether, and to what extent, we per-
onally and collectively cling to Christ's redeeming grace.

11

A Voice from the Byzantine East

We have the dubious consolation of being able to state th[
no Church, no Christian group, has been indifferent to the cause
Christian unity. Granted, we have not always taken proper measur
to bring unity about (and sometimes, we have even tried to fin
comfort in our isolation). Yet whenever circumstances have place
the Churches in confrontation with this problem, Bishops, Pope
and Patriarchs have always proclaimed that they desire uni
because Christ desired it and even prayed for it.

For some time now, this wish or desire has given place
restlessness. It was no sudden, thoughtless improvisation on Pop
John XXIII's part, but the climax of several decades of work an
prayer coming from Christians the world over. Pope John mere
voiced the unanimous hope for unity when he called for a univers
Synod of Roman Catholic Bishops to assemble in Rome in 1962. F
wished to begin the work of restoring unity. The response of th
Christian world to his call was unanimous; it was like the reply of
single soul, so long burdened by a serious sin, to whom the mean
for lifting that sin had just been extended. Both leaders and peop
of the world-wide Christian communities responded immediate
and affirmatively, while nurturing the hope that a viable unity wou
not be far off.

Both the Churches and the Church want unity, but there ar
of course, men in every Christian denomination - a minority, to t
sure - who do not desire it. Some believe that the other parties a
not holy enough to be joined with them. Some find the others amb
tious for wanting everything and everyone; proud, for daring to trea
them as brothers. Some might judge a union superfluous since the
themselves, are already in the Church; indeed, since they have ofte
been told that the Church is the members, they would prefer it t
remain confined to its present membership, namely themselves.

These men reduce the Church of Christ to their own specif
cations and cannot find in it any room for others. Furthermore, the
reduce truth to the limitations of their own minds, color it with the
own peculiarities, and term as error every other facet of that sam
Truth. Indeed, is this not the real reason for the continued separa
tion of the Eastern and Western Churches - the failure of each t
recognize the other's legitimate ecclesiastical tradition?

The evil one has ever sown men like these throughout Chris
tendom. They are to be found in every Church, in every period c
history. They, themselves, are often unaware of the evil they ar
doing, but the evil is there, nonetheless. For centuries they hav

ndered even the most minor steps toward unity and today they
em bent on compromising the strides taken by the Second Vatican
ouncil and by the World Council of churches. These disciples of
scord present the progress toward unity achieved by both these
oups as something less than it is: The manifestation of God's
agnificent plan.

We would like to point out to them that Pope John XXIII, in
unching his appeal for unity, had no ulterior motive. He was not
inking of personal gain or seeking Catholic superiority. He merely
iced the unanimous longing of all the Christian people.

A few examples of mankind's longing for unity are to be
en in interdenominational meetings, frequent contacts, ecumeni-
l dialogue, interconfessional gatherings, united social action and
int prayer, especially during Unity Week. These occurrences have
eadily advanced the cause and have prepared the Christian world
honor it, to achieve it, and to warmly welcome it. It is no longer
ly man's right to place his own meaning on the Second Vatican
ouncil's progress or on the numerous moves toward perfect unity
ken by the World Council of Churches.

No Church has the right to announce its hostility to the
ppeal to unity merely because the appeal has come from the Pope
f Rome any more than the Catholic Church would have the option
be deaf to the same appeal had it come from the humblest of its
ithful or from another Christian leader. The Pope has not created
e problem of disunity, and therefore, can claim no monopoly on it.
is a dilemma facing every soul living in grace.

The Christian Church is not the private or exclusive property
f any one man or group of men. When the Pope calls for re-union
r summons a council to discuss this problem, he is not inviting
hristians to come and partake of his own heritage; but to Jesus
hrist, their only Savior, for "there is only one God, and only one
ediator between God and men, Jesus Christ" (I Timothy 2:5).

Every Christian bishop and every member of the faithful
wes it to his brothers and sisters to contribute in his fullest mea-
ure to the realization of Christ's yearning "that all may be one".
his unity is God's good, it is the good of our Lord, and it is for the
ood and the beauty of each and every Christian soul. Why?
ecause in a united Church everyone will benefit from an over-
bundance of graces and be made beautiful by the graces flowing
om above.

It is clear then that any man who would set himself up
gainst the efforts leading to an undivided Church, no matter

whence his efforts come, would be sinning against the Son of G
and the people He came to unite. Would he not, also, be sinni
against the whole of mankind, called to faith in Christ Jesus? How
this so? Simply because the non-believer is looking to see "how t
Christians love one another" but he finds division among them.

Anyone, Catholic, Orthodox, Anglican, Protestant or wha
ever: anyone who has become complacent during the centuries
separation for no matter what reason, that person is using himself
obstruct the progress of unity! "He who is not with Me, is agair
Me" (Matt. 12-30) applies here. For this he will be severely judg
on the last day! We contend that these men are doing within t
Churches what sin does within the soul. They must first remove th
imperfection if they desire to contribute to the realization of O
Lord's yearning: "Father, may they all be One, as you and I a
One."

Notes

1. The theme behind Prince Myshkin's words in Dostoievsky's *T.
Idiot*: "only Beauty will save the world," permeates this essay. On
interpretation of this is that Zoghby appears to equate perfe
beauty with the unity of men and the union of Churches. [R.B.]

2. This theme appears in a meditation by the late Thomas Merton
Conjectures of a Guilty Bystander, Doubleday-Image Books editio
Garden City, N.Y., 1968,p. 21. [R.B.]

3. Ronald Knox translation of the Holy Bible. The Knox translatio
will be used in this chapter alone. [R.B.]

4. It is clear that Archbishop Zoghby believes, along with Vladin
Soloviev, that man is something higher than Augustinian and oth
Catholic (let alone Lutheran and the various Protestants) theolo;
envisions him to be. Man is potentially divine, as Soloviev taugl
and it is his human vocation and destiny to approximate God eve
while in this world! [R.B.]

Two - The Unity and Diversity of the Church

The Church is the bride of Jesus Christ and is the work of the Holy Trinity. Just as man has been made in God's image and likeness and reflects God's activity by his knowledge and love, so too the Church, the continuation of Jesus Christ on this planet, should be manifestation in time of the life of the Trinity. In the first instance there is the epiphany (i.e. manifestation) of God the Creator of man; in the second there is the epiphany of God, one and yet three, through Christ and the Church: "As the Father has sent Me, I send you in the same manner." (John 20: 21)

"Then all those every tribe and tongue, people and nation (cf. Rev. 5: 9) who have been redeemed by the blood of Christ and gathered into one Church, with one song of praise magnify the one and triune God."[1]

The Triune God is but one in its Trinity; multiple humanity, yet one in its diversity, in its universality and in its catholicity. "Father, that they may be one as We are one" (John 17: 22) but with this difference: it is the one God who, by knowledge and love, is triune; on the contrary, it is the universality of men who, by their knowledge and love of the Son of God, must constitute the One Church. If we wish to see the survival of this planet we must succeed in making all men united in the faith and knowledge of the Son of God.

Paragraph 23 of the *Constitution on the Church* says: "By divine Providence it has come about that various churches established in diverse places by the Apostles and their successors have in the course of time coalesced into several groups, organically united, which, preserving the unity of faith and the unique divine constitution of the universal Church, enjoy their own discipline, their own liturgical usage, and their own theological and spiritual heritage... This variety of local churches with one common aspiration is particularly splendid evidence of the catholicity of the undivided Church."

The Trinity in God is constituted by the fact that each Divine Person is a *relation* to the others. The Father is entirely ordered to the Son; the Son entirely ordered - one might say consecrated - to the Father; and, at least according to one Eastern Christian tradition, the Holy Spirit is the emanation of the Father through the Son.

"Father, that they may be one as We are One."(John 17: 22) All men, coming from the hand of God, should always be able to know and love one another, so that the human family might always be united, always one, in fact as well as in theory. But sin has made men unaccommodating to each other: neither their common origin, nor their natural brotherhood, nor the material advantages of unity have been strong enough to unite them permanently. Boundaries have always been drawn between nations and wars have always set them against each other. We experience the truth of the saying: "*Homo homini lupus.*" Men could not be united in their first father Adam because of his sin. There had to be another unifier, a second Adam, and this, which was realized in Jesus, was made manifest to us particularly in His Incarnation and Resurrection, the two great mysteries effecting our resurrection, our redemption and the renewal of all created things. "And the Word was made flesh," the writer of John's first gospel tells us, "to gather into one the children of God who are scattered."(John 11: 52)

Unity in Christ

The God-Man is not just the mediator, the intermediary of unity; he is its source and its center. He must in Himself unite the scattered children of God.

"The Son... came on the mission from His Father. It was in Him, before the foundation of the world, that the Father chose us and predestined us to become adopted sons, for in Him it has pleased the Father to re-establish all things (cf. Ephesians 1, 4-5 and 10)." (#3)

This unity must be accomplished in His Body which is the Church: "The head of this body is Christ; He is the image of the invisible God and in Him all things came into being... He had priority over everyone and in Him all things hold together. He is the head of that Body, which is the Church."(#7)

Now this Body will not realize its fullness without us. For it is by building up this Body, that is, by uniting ourselves to it by becoming one with Him, that we will bring forth the complete Christ, which is Jesus and us together, Jesus and the Church united into one.

This integration of ourselves into Christ, which is the condition of our deepest life and of our unity, is the work of the Holy Spirit: "Christ has given us His Spirit Who, one and the same in the head and in the members, gives life, unity and movement to the entire body." (#7)

Building Up and Uniting the Church

To build up the Church is to unite it. For just as the human body of Christ was not born as a full-grown adult, the same holds true of the Church. The Church must *become* an adult. St. Paul, when writing to the Ephesians tells them and all Christians that the ministry has been entrusted to the Apostles, prophets, evangelists, pastors and teachers "for building up the Body of Christ until we all attain the unity of the faith and the knowledge of the Son of God and consti-tute the perfect man, who in mature manhood reaches the fullness of Christ." (Eph 4: 11-13) In other words, in spite of our differences, all of us must become one. How? By together building up the Mystical Body of Christ.[2] The Church must not only build up peoples, but by integrating them allow itself to be constructed by them until it attains the stature of the perfect man, the fullness of Christ,. The whole of humanity must then build up the Church, not merely be received into the Church. Otherwise, it will nei-ther be part of the Church nor will it be integrated into the Body of Christ.

Unity is not just a gift or a quality superimposed upon the church. The Church is united as it is built up. By his acceptance of the Church, each person becomes a stone in the construction. "In the Church we here on earth are being built up as living stones."(#6) It is by bringing together these stones, by uniting or consolidating them, that we con-struct that edifice of the Church. It is by uniting in faith, in knowledge and love of Jesus that men construct the Body of Christ. To put it another way, the Church is united to the extent that it is being built up; and the Church will not be completed until she had adopted all men and that will take place at the end of time: "Foreshadowed from the beginning of the world... [the Church] will be consummated in glory at the end of time." (#2)

The unity of the Church then is not something to be accomplished (by men) once and for all; it must be won day by day until the end of time. Each of us has to struggle all his life to make or to maintain the unity of his own being in spite of the diversity of the tendencies of his body and soul, emotions and intellect. By this struggle he supports and develops his inmost life. Once united, the Church, too, must preserve its members in unity drawing together and integrating those who are outside of her by a continual effort of renunciation, of charity and of service which is the normal means for the Church to build herself up and to deepen her life. When we pray and work for unity we do not mean just settling down into a tranquil unity but rather obtaining the grace to live it, to deepen it and to keep constructing it all the days of our life. And since the unity between us is connected with our union with Christ we cannot, once united in Him, be permanently established in grace, that is to say, in union with Christ, as long as we live on this earth. If the Church, being desirous of this unity, stopped working toward it as if it were already possessed, the Church would cease to build itself up, and by this very fact it would cease to live. We must not only achieve unity, but keep it, maintain it, in diversity, just as we have to struggle to keep the state of grace and unity with God within ourselves. "Apply yourselves," says the Apostle Paul to the Ephesians, "to maintain the unity of the Spirit by the bond of peace." (Eph. 4: 3) For this reason we pray in every Eucharistic Liturgy: "Preserve the fullness (i.e. the members, etc.) of Your Church..."

To preserve unity, to live it every day, is constantly to adhere to Jesus Christ that we see Him alone in everything: "No, I did not wish to know anything from among you except Jesus Christ and Him crucified." (I Cor. 2: 2) Jesus Christ then is all in all. Neither can incompatibility of personalities nor racial, cultural, national or social differences, neither time nor distance, divide those who love each other in Christ. Every Christian must put on Christ and in Him each other in Christ. Every Christian must put on Christ in Him each man disappears under His Divine countenance. "You who have been baptized in Christ have put on Christ" as a garment, we see in Paul's letter to the Galatians; "now there is neither Jew nor Greek, neither slave nor free, neither male nor female; for you all have been made one in Christ Jesus." (Gal. 3: 27-29) Again, "there is only one Body and one Spirit, only one Lord, one faith, one baptism, one God and Father of all, through all and all." (Ephesians 4: 4-6) Only one Spirit, one Lord, and one God and Father of all. "So the entire Church appears as the people united in the unity of the Father, the Son and the Holy Spirit," (#4)

Unity Patterned After the Trinity

The unity of the Divine Persons and the participation of each Christian in their intimate life must be both the model and the source of Christian unity: "That they may be one, just as You, Father, are in Me and I am in You, let them also be one in us so that the world may believe that You have sent Me." (John 17: 20-21) The unity of believers must have for its pattern, its exemplary cause, the unity of the Father and the Son. "As You, Father, are in Me, and I an in You." But this is not all. Christian unity must have its source in this unity of the Father and Son: "That they may be one in Us." *As us*... and *in us*. "So the entire Church will appear as the people united with the unity of the Father and the Son and the Holy Spirit." (#4) Then Christian unity will be for the world the most excellent witness of the Divine mission of Jesus Christ and of the unity which exists between the Father and Him: "So that the world may believe that You have sent Me."

Modeled after the Trinity and accomplished in the Trinity, Christian unity must participate in the modalities of Trinitarian unity. "You must believe," He said to His Apostles, "that I am the Father and the Father is in Me." (John 14: 11) Everywhere that the Son is present, the Father is also present and also the Trinity. The three Divine Persons are distinct, but the triune God is indivisible. The Church of Jesus Christ, one in its diversity, must in its own way share in this indivisibility. The Church universal is comprised of all

19

the local Churches, but the local Church is present in each parish. *The Constitution on the Church* clearly states: "This Church of Christ is truly present in all the legitimate congregations of the faithful. Joined with their pastors, these groups are called churches in the New Testament. For in their own locality they are the new people called by God in the Holy Spirit and in much fullness (cf. I Thess. 1: 5)... In these communities, although frequently small and poor or rather isolated, Christ is present. Through this presence, the Church, one, holy, catholic and apostolic, is gathered together." (#26)

The entire Church of Jesus Christ (with bishops, priests and faithful, with all the treasures of divine life and all the graces of the Redemption) is present at the smallest altar in the tiniest country village when a priest, in union with the local bishop, celebrates the Eucharist there. Thus the smallest church of the smallest parish can be proud of being able to say to the Church of Jesus Christ: "I am in You and You in Me... Everything which is Mine is Yours, and everything that is Yours is Mine." And the most humble priest (united with his bishop and thus to the Church) can dispense at the altar all the treasures of the Redemption entrusted by Christ to His Church: Jesus Christ, His Cross, and His glory.

Unity Through the Eucharist

It is at the altar in the Eucharistic celebration that the work of unity is, in fact, accomplished and perpetuated "until He comes." "Truly sharing in the Body of the Lord in the braking of the Eucharistic bread, we are brought into communion with Him and with each other." (#7) Christian unity is not only a unity in faith; it is most especially a union in life, in the common participation in the divine life. But it is by participation in the Eucharistic sacrifice of the Cross, that men throughout time can share in the fruits of the Redemption and be nourished in this life at the same source, Jesus Christ. Just as the Cross of Jesus is the center of unity of men with Christ (cf. "when I am lifted up from the earth, I will draw all things to Myself," John 12: 32), the altar of the Eucharistic sacrifice is likewise the center of the unity of

Christians with Christ and with each other. Vatican II's *Constitution on the Church* recalls this when it refers to the first letter to the Corinthians: "Every time that the sacrifice of the Cross, in which Christ, our Passover, has been sacrificed (I Cor. 5: 7), is celebrated on the altar, the work of our redemption is accomplished. At this time, the unity of the faithful, who constitute one Body in Christ (cf. I Cor. 10: 17), is both signified and accomplished by the sacrament of the Eucharistic bread."(#3)

The Eucharist, then, is the bond between the faithful and the Church. But this is not all. It is the Eucharist itself which brings about the presence of the Church in the world. It makes the Church effectively and completely present in all places where it is celebrated. It is then at the altar that the Church appears as a mystery of communion; it is there that it achieves its essential unity, despite the obstacles that men place in the way.

Our Lord commanded His followers to love one another as He had loved them (John 13: 34), that is, with the same love with which He loved them. But Christ's love for mankind reached its peak on the Cross, for can there be any greater love than to give one's life for those he loves? (cf. John 15: 14) If then we must love one another with the same love with which Jesus loves us, it is around the altar, the continuation of Calvary that we must gather "in a mystical way," as the Byzantine Liturgy states, to let ourselves be filled with love of Jesus Christ, that love which we must have for one another. This love, given us to eat and drink under the forms of bread and wine, is to enable us to complete within us the sacrifice of our Savior and Victim. It was by eating the victims that the people of old, and even some aborigines living today, completed their sacrifices. It was especially by letting themselves be devoured by the beasts or by fire that the first Christians completed their sacrifices of themselves. Did not the Martyr and Archbishop of Antioch, St. Ignatius, hope to be ground up and pulverized by the teeth of the animals in order to become the wheat of Jesus Christ, just as Christ in the Eucharist had become the purest wheat for the faithful? It is by eating the Body of the Savior and drinking His Blood that we become one with Him and, being one with Him, we are necessarily one in Him. This is what St. Paul meant when he wrote to the Corinthians: "The cup of blessing which we bless, is it not fellowship in the Blood of Christ? The Bread which we break, is it not fellowship in the Body of Christ? Since there is only one bread, we, though many, form only one body since we all share in the one bread. Consider the practice of Israel: Are not those who eat the victim partners in the altar?" (I Cor. 10: 16-19) By sharing in this same bread, we all become members of this Body (cf. I Cor. 12: 27) and "individually members of one another." (Rom. 12: 5) "And nourished by the Body of Christ in His Holy assembly, the faithful manifest in a concrete manner the unity of the people of God which is suitably signified and wondrously accomplished by the most awesome sacrament." (#11)

Since Christ loves us by giving us His flesh as food, and we must love one another with this same love, it is not possible for us to make our eucharistic communion into a private action which begins and ends with us. Instead the Eucharistic Liturgy must be a community action *par excellence*, an "intercommunion which allows us to mutually give Christ to one another by means of His own love with which we love one another. So each of us will be able to say of his brother at the same time (and also, simultaneously of Jesus, our Divine Brother): "He loved me and delivered himself up for me." (Gal. 2: 20) Thus Christ's powerful love for our brothers, by coming to them through us, will also bring them our complete, transformed, powerful and unselfish love. By thus receiving the Body and Blood of Christ we have communion with each other, giving our "blood" with His Blood. How supremely beautiful and how truly eucharistic was the saying of the holy priest Chevrier who, in order to express the total gift that the priest makes of himself for mankind, said: "the priest is a consumed man."

Universality, a Condition for Unity

The Eucharist, as we have seen, is the sacrament of unity *par excellence*, uniquely unlike and above all other sacraments. But in order not to degenerate into mere conformity, unity must respect diversity and universality. This universality is three-fold: universality of peoples, of traditions, and of the governmental systems.

Psychologists and sociologists rightly inform us that the condition of one's birth has such an influence on both that particular individual and those around him that it is impossible for him to live without detriment to himself unless this fact (i.e. the fact that everyone is different) is recognized and provision is made for it. This is also true of the Church, born on Pentecost in the midst of a huge throng of various races, customs and languages. After Peter's discourse, this same group was united in the same faith and by the same baptism. The author of the Acts of the Apostles relates what happened: "There were, residing in Jerusalem, devout men from every nation under heaven. Hearing these things, the multitude was amazed, for each one heard the apostles speaking in his own language ... Parthians, Medes and Elamites, inhabitants of Mesopotamia, Judea and Cappadocia, of Pontus and Asia, of Phrygia and Pamphylia, of Egypt and the part of Libya near Cyrene, visitors from Rome, both Jews and proselytes, Cretans and Arabians - we have heard them in our own language telling of the marvellous works of God." (Acts 2: 5-11) It was in this setting of universality that God had planned and also accomplished the birth of His Church, and it is in that same type of setting that He wants it to live. The Church must receive all peoples with equality; she must preach the same faith and the same baptism but in their own national and cultural language and according to their peculiar character and mentality. No obstacle must prevent the Church from reaching all peoples and being established in every inhabited area and land throughout the world. Nothing, no, nothing must prevent this, not language, color, location, differences of mentality, nationality or culture, race, or anything else. "The multitude of believers," whose diverse origins the author of the Acts just mentioned, was "of one heart and one mind," (Acts 4: 32) and this is all that is necessary to belong to Christ's Church. The day that the Church cuts itself off from this universality and tries to become the personal domain of some "chosen" people and of some definite country, it really renounces its universality and becomes a mere local and particular Church. The uniformity of human activity would then be substituted for the unity first made manifest at Pentecost and destined to continue throughout time in the Church universal.

In itself, however, the multiplicity of races, colors, languages, etc., is not sufficient for the Church to be called universal or catholic. A powerful and generous Church can still enlist members from all nations, allow them to pray in their own language and still not ever emerge from its own particularism. To be universal then, the Church must not only make all peoples its own but must itself become part of them. The new Churches must find in the universal Church the transfiguration of their own particular human heritage; their civilization, their heritage and traditions, that which constitutes their unique spirit must be integrated into their new life in Christ's Church. The ancient Churches, apostolic or nearly apostolic, must have been conscious of this, otherwise we would not have so many rites and theologies in the main Christian Churches today, particularly in the East. Today, it is not necessary that only the East be aware of this; the West must be attentive to this quality also, and must apply this to its new branches and to awaken it in many other sections of its patriarchate. Returning to the case of the neophyte bodies however, we should keep in mind that their Christian heritage, their legitimate religious traditions and their human civilization, enriched by them throughout many centuries under the guidance of the Holy Spirit, must be integrated into the Church on an equal basis, without any distinction due to race, social conditions or even numbers of their faithful.

The application of quantitative and numerical standards to the supernatural order is often the great temptation to the catholicity of the Church. As Western Christians themselves admit, the Greek and Eastern Christian heritage form the richest and most authentic part of Christian tradition; yet it is represented by only a few million faithful in the midst of the Catholic Church of Rome which numbers several hundred million people. It is this numerical fact which constantly tempts the Catholic Church to think of herself and act as if she were a Latin, Western Church exclusively.

Furthermore, in the midst of the two great Christian traditions of the East and the West there is a great variety of peoples and civilizations to which should correspond a variety of legitimate religious traditions. But why are there so many diverse traditions in Eastern Christianity and so few in the West? Because the universality of ecclesiastical traditions can be created and maintained only in a diversity of responsible ecclesiastical bodies. The universality of the Christian heritage and its very integrity presupposes and even demands the universality of its government as well as its unity, and that is the type of diversity (in directing bodies) such as has always been found in the Christian East.

Every Church governed, either locally or from a distance, by men who are foreign to its traditions will progressively but certainly adopt the traditions of those who govern it.[3] This occurs to the detriment of the local Church's own traditions and makes it a foreigner even in its own land. The Second Vatican Council's restoration to the bishops of complete power over there own local Churches is of great importance to assure the Church's universality, the very condition of its unity. We note, parenthetically and with displeasure, that the Roman Curia is still doing all in its power to withhold these legitimate powers *of divine right* from the bishops as it has similarly prevented the Eastern Catholic Churches from using all their rightful powers and privileges.[4] But this episcopal power, lest it degenerates into provincialism and begins to limit its outlook to local matters and thereby compromise the unity of the Church, must be complemented by the collegial power of the episcopate over the whole Church, also a power of divine right. It is exercised by means of either ecumenical councils or episcopal conferences.

Collegiality has always been strong in the East due to the presence of the many apostolic sees conscious of their task in the Church and working together under the rule of the Patriarchal Synod. The Synod, while not preventing the local Churches from developing normally and according to their own authentic regional traditions, maintains by its very nature a unity excluding uniformity. On the other hand, ecclesiastical government in the West has become more centralized around the West's single apostolic see of Rome. Gradually, the bishop of Rome, who was both the Patriarch of the West and the first bishop of Christianity, took the governing of the entire Latin Church into his own hands.[5] One diocese, one people, and only one tradition (and a local one at that), foisted its spirit, its law, and its Roman characteristics on the entire West. Obviously, such a centralization could not favor the growth or development of local traditions.

The evolution of each human group is fashioned by its own particular temperament, spirit, mentality and the local conditions of its life. Just as culture proceeds slowly and normally, integration with and fusion with the specific milieu - insofar as it is possible, and so long as the Church does not compromise truth - must be a gradual process. Evolution of this kind will allow for full expression of the verities of the universal faith in the local idiom.

When the natural way, outlined above, is not followed, submission to a specified religious rule imposed from outside takes place. Being unnatural, it creates a dichotomy in the people between their thought and religious life on the one hand, and their natural and human evolution on the other. This difficulty provokes religious crises. The Vatican Council's *Constitution on the Church*, when defining the power of the episcopacy, considers the exercise of collegial episcopal power through episcopal conferences as being legitimate. By declaring this, the Second Vatican Council restored to each priest and to every one of the faithful his full place in the Mystical Body of Christ. It gave back to each local Church the possibility of governing itself and of maintaining its religious life in harmony with the conditions of its human life. This is a new reformation. This time it was accomplished, thanks be to God, within the Church and by the Church herself.

A well known saying states that good financial arrangements make good friends. Why should we hesitate to apply this proverb (with qualifications, of course) to the relations between religious groups? Good understanding between Churches, as well as their unity, cannot be maintained by any means that would prove detrimental to "good arrangements." People's good will and their hope for spiritual rewards can lead them to temporarily accept a form of government within the Church that might actually be incompatible with their temperament and life style. If, however, nature is placed into some artificial opposition to grace, nature will eventually stake a claim to its legitimate rights and demand a correction of those affairs. A just distribution of rights in all phases of life, even in the religious, is necessary to peoples and to the churches so that they can remain " good friends" and live together in peace and unity.

The Role of Collegiality and Primacy

Some might believe that collegiality and primacy are two distinct gifts from God to His Church: the first to keep its catholicity or universality, and the second to preserve its unity. It is a serious mistake to so believe. Since the universal Church is made up of the totality of all the Churches or dioceses, the unity of the universal Church must be of the order as that which each Church, each diocese enjoys. The foundation and bond of this unity in the universal Church therefore, must not be foreign to the foundation and the bond of unity which exists in each local (diocesan) Church.

The unity of each diocese is founded upon Jesus Christ, preserved in His grace and joined together in the same faith and the same Eucharist. It cannot be otherwise in the universal Church. In addition, since the visible bond of unity in each diocese is its own bishop, the assembly or college of bishops can not be foreign to the unity of the universal Church (unless the Bishop of Rome is also the bishop of each diocese, which he is not). Therefore, the college of bishops which assures the Church's catholicity or universality is itself the visible bond of its unity, provided that it is united to its temporal head, the bishop of Rome who is both the head and, at the same time, the unifying bond of the episcopal college. "In order that the episcopacy itself might be one and indivisible, Jesus Christ has placed the blessed Peter at the head of the other apostles." (#18) Thus, the unity of the Church has its source, its foundation, in Jesus Christ, head of the Church and principle of its divine life. It has its visible link in the Bishop of Rome, not as an authority isolated from the other bishops, but only inasmuch as he is head of the episcopal college and the bond of its unity, as the Constitution on the Church states with clarity: "Each individual bishop is the visible principle and foundation of unity in his particular church, formed to the image of the universal Church, in which and from which exists the one and unique Catholic Church. Thus each individual bishop represents his church, and all the bishops together with the Pope, represent the entire Church in the bond of peace, love and unity." (#23)

Now we can understand why authentic collegiality, not merely lip-service collegiality, is necessary if the Church desires to undertake a dialog with the scattered children of God. To be effective, even to be possible, this dialog must be undertaken in each locality by the bishops, in cooperation and in collaboration with their priests and faithful. Any dialog which restricts itself only to the top level is doomed to failure, for men, especially in the area of religion, are not sheep who will blindly follow some leader without knowing the whys or the wherefores. Since Christian unity must be brought about in Jesus Christ, it must become the work of every man who lives in Jesus Christ. The dialog, however, cannot be undertaken only on the local or diocesan level, for this would only bring about local agreements that would remain isolated and without efficacy for the unity of all mankind. The dialog must be undertaken on all levels of human society: parochial, diocesan, national, regional and universal. From this arises the necessity of episcopal conference, councils and a central government.

Legalism as a Foundation for Unity

There are three false foundations - commonly proposed yet useless to follow - for the building of Christian unity: they are legalism, paternalism, and particularism.

The unity of the Church must not be seen principally under the aspect of legal authority. Unity of government is necessary of course, but it is not the one chief thing; most especially, it is not the only unity willed by Our Lord. We must ever keep before our eyes the idea that Christian unity resides primarily and essentially in the realm of the interior life, the life of grace, and in this way, in the union of its members with one another and, at the same time, with Jesus Christ who is the head of the Church. Therefore, this unity is essentially the work of the Spirit working through love. "In the building up of Christ's body, there is a diversity of members and of functions ... It is the Spirit who gives the Body its unity through Himself and by His power and by the intimate joining of its members. Thus this same Spirit produces and increases the love between the faithful." (#7)

The government of the Church is directed toward this mysterious unity as a means to the end, just as the Church, the Kingdom of God upon earth and an imperfect kingdom, is directed toward the heavenly, perfect Kingdom. The Church Militant is not permanent; it will not be transferred to heaven in its present framework and with a hierarchy familiar to us. Rather, each person will have to give an individual account of his life and will occupy in the Church Triumphant the place which his works have merited. In heaven, as Jesus Himself told us, many among the last will be the first, and many among the first will be the last. "The Church, to which we are all called in Jesus Christ and in which, by the Grace of God, we achieve holiness, will only be completed in the glory of heaven." (#48)

The government of the Church, its structure, its hierarchy, will vanish with the world. Only our union with God will remain and will be the measure of our eternal happiness. But in the hierarchy of values, we must give priority on earth to what will remain eternally and yet not neglect anything. For example, let us consider the theological virtues of faith, hope and love. All three are indispensable for salvation. But faith and hope will not have any reason to exist after death when one sees God face to face, for faith will yield to the vision of God and hope to the possession of God, who is Himself love. Since love never ends (cf. I Cor. 13, 8), it is this love which will comprise our everlasting life, for we will then possess God and see Him directly, face to face, and being in love with Him for all eternity and He with each of us! This love will unify the heavenly Church forever, this love which will permanently gather the scattered children of God around His Son. Therefore the unity of the people of God on earth must be considered first and foremost as love. And even though some men of goodwill do not share our faith in a visible way, they do share our love and are still included in the Kingdom of God.

Charity and love, that is union by grace to Jesus Christ, is the purpose of the Incarnation and Redemption. The sacraments are the supernatural means chosen by God to introduce, maintain and develop this love in our souls. Of these sacraments the Eucharist in particular must occupy a choice place in the work of unity because not only is it a unifying bond but it is a sacrament of love. But since the sacraments still remain only a means, we know that God who chose them can give men who happen to be ignorant of them (the sacraments) other means to acquire and preserve this love and thus to be integrated into the Kingdom of God.

The purpose for ecclesiastical government is the maintenance and regulation of good order that will insure the proper performance of the sacraments so that we may benefit from it and may regulate and maintain our sacramental life. It is a means designed principally to organize the administration of the sacraments, which are themselves only a means to an end. "Until there is the new heaven and the new earth where justice dwells (2 Peter 3: 13), the pilgrim Church in its sacraments and institutions which belong to this world takes on the appearance of this passing world."(#48) The juridical organizations which must assure this government of the Church are necessary, but only a means. They must never permit the Church to view itself as an end to itself, for the Church's only *raison d'etre* is *Diakonia*, service, and it must not be permitted to forget it!

Thus it is a great error to see Christian unity primarily as a juridical unity. The predominant role we often, but mistakenly, attribute to juridical unity seems to arise from the temptation of the Church to look upon its provisional organizations, hierarchical structure and canonical legislation as an end in itself rather than as a means. And when the means is changed into an end, it assumes a character of necessity, of rigidity and of intransigence which compromises the end for which it was established. Although the end is of its very nature stable and unchanging, the means must be flexible and adaptable by its nature.

If a Church tries above all to become fixed in its earthly structure and to establish, as on Mount Tabor, a tent to its Master in which the passing glory of the Transfiguration can be fixed, then this Church risks turning in on itself, forgetting that we are a pilgrim Church and that "we do not have a permanent city here on earth, but we look for that which is to come."(Hebrews 13: 14) Tabor is not heaven; it is merely its fleeting image. In our ecclesiastical structure we do not encompass the Kingdom of God on earth. The mystical Body of Jesus Christ is not constituted only by the baptized who are juridically subject to the visible government of the Church. All men of good will who live in the state of holy grace are part of it. "All the just since Adam, from Abel the just to the last of the elect, will be gathered together around the Father in the universal Church."(#1) Furthermore, the inspired writer tells us that "at all times and in every nation, he who fears God and practices justice is pleasing to God (cf. Acts 10: 35)."(#9)

Paternalism as a Foundation for Unity

According to Scripture, the unity of the Church does not principally consist in the meeting of its juridical government. By forgetting this people often confuse the Church with the men in the Church. No matter how high in the ranks of the hierarchy, men have their narrowness, their peculiarities, their own individual character traits whether these be hereditary or acquired. When these men are confused with the Church, when they themselves become the Church, then this Church which Christ intended should have a divine dimension - a Church "splendid, without stain or wrinkle or anything of the sort, but holy and immaculate"(Eph. 5: 27) - this Church takes on their own troubles and their personal, familial and national limits. But we know that men and nations are so different and at the same time so affected by original sin that alone they are incapable of accomplishing the unity of the human race. As a matter of fact, ever since creation mankind has never ceased to be divided, as history demonstrates. Only Jesus Christ can accomplish this unity between men. He has chosen to accomplish it through the Church and in the Church, provided that we Christians accept our role as merely instruments in His hands and provided that He Himself remains the Alpha and the Omega of His Church. But if this Church, patterned itself after earthly societies, becomes inspired by the workings of human power alone, it begins to be identified with one man or a group of men or some particular nation (as it once was identified with the Empire), and then it will submit to the spirit of domination and to imperialism which takes on the outward appearance of paternalism in order to appear as love. From this point on, dialogue based on equality can not be undertaken either with the Churches or with the world. Universality cannot then be realized and, for the most part, unity will be compromised.

The *Constitution on the Church* affirms this very well: "Although by the will of Christ certain men are established to be teachers over others, dispensers of the mysteries, and pastors, there reigns among men a true equality as to their dignity and as to the work of building up the body of Christ which is common to all the faithful ... So just as the laity have Christ for their brother because of God's graciousness ... so too the laity have for their brothers those who work in the sacred ministry, teaching, sanctifying, ruling and shepherding the family of God by the authority of Christ. As St. Augustine beautifully put in, "I am terrified to be for you and consoled to be among you: terrified to be a bishop for you, consoled by being a Christian. The first title is an obligation; the second is a grace. The former is a danger; the latter, salvation."(#32)

God Himself would not want a unity undertaken under the protection and guise of protection of paternalism. "Yahweh is called jealous, for He is a jealous God." (Exodus 34:14) "But you," He said to His disciples, "are not to let anyone call you Rabbi, since you have only one Master and you are all brothers. Do not call anyone on earth your Father, for you have only one Father, who is in heaven. Do not let anyone call you teacher, for you have only one teacher, Christ. For the greatest among you must be your servant." (Matt. 23: 8-12)

"And that duty, which the Lord committed to the shepherds of His people, is a true service which the Scriptures significantly call *diakonia* or "a ministry of service" (cf. Acts 1: 17, 25; Romans 11: 13; I Timothy 1: 12)" (24)

If the Church wants to attain Christian and human unity, it must not be identified with any one man or group of men. It must be available, free of any tutelage and all human condescension in order to adopt in equality all mankind in Jesus Christ. By the same token, those whom Christ has established as the foundation and pillars of His Church deserve the respect of the faithful. They deserve the trust and attachment due to Jesus Christ Himself who said: "Whoever hears you, hears Me; and whoever despises you, despises Me." Luke 22: 26) Jesus promised them that He would "be with them even unto the consummation of the world." (Matt. 28: 20) But at the same time He commanded humility and renunciation to one another: "Whoever is the leader must conduct himself as one who serves." (Luke 22: 26) The role of the Apostle is that of a delegate or a steward. He must not take the place of the Master. St. Paul wrote to the Corinthians: "We must be seen as servants of Christ and stewards of the mysteries of God." (I Cor. 4:1) "No one should glorify himself in men for, neither Paul or Apollo or Cephas, they are all your servants. Now you belong to Christ and Christ belongs to God." (I Cor. 3: 21-23) Paternalism is in some way substituting someone else for the Father who is God; it is trying to lead others to us, rather then leading them to God as servants should. The apostle of Jesus Christ must be the bearer of Christ, a *Christophoros*. His role is, in a certain sense, "eucharistic." When Christ becomes present in the bread, it loses its own essence. The bread just retains its appearances, but is no longer bread. All veneration, all adoration before the host or lamb is not to the bread itself (which exists only under its appearances) but really to Jesus Christ, hidden under the sign of bread. So it should be with men of the Church: emptied of themselves, they will lead the world to Christ, the only mediator, to the only Father, the Father of Jesus and our Father. "All are your servants, but you belong to Christ and Christ belongs to God."

Particularism as a Foundation for Unity

Historically speaking, divisions within the Church have been caused by the universal Church retreating into one of its parts. Each time the Church has wanted to identify herself with one local tradition, one school of theological thought. In other words, each time the entire Church has wanted to identify itself with a particular Church, a break has taken place. It has often been by the choice of one particular theological formula to the exclusion of another that many churches have been separated and have remained separated for centuries. The Church then discovered, but unfortunately too late, that most of the different formulas were not opposed, that the so-called monophysite opinion was not denying Chalcedon, that the Latin *filioque* did not directly contradict the traditions of the Orthodox Eastern Church.[6] Was is not the too hasty identification of the interests of the Latin Church with those of the *whole* Church and the identification of the interests of the Christian West with those of the universal Catholic Church that produce the Great Christian Schism, unjustly called the Eastern Schism? This schism opposed two particular Churches, the Latin and the Greek, but was viewed by the Western Church as a schism between the Eastern Church and the universal Church. I take the liberty of citing one of my speeches at the third session of the Second Vatican Council: "The universal Church is made up of all the particular Churches, gathered together by the Holy Spirit and organized from the first centuries around the great sees. The principal and most effective of these was the one at Rome because she received the consent of all (to be the chief Church) and because of the apostolic succession of the see of Peter, permanently established there. But this universal Church must not be exclusively identified with "universality" of the Western and Latin Church. This specific Church only began to exist as a separate entity at a later date, notably during the reign of Charlemagne, and grew little by little, due to and taking advantage of the fact that it was separated from the East. One day it found itself all alone though, having forgotten the ancient patriarchal structure of the Church ... Easterners, however, have always kept the original conception and achieved that practical pluralism which His Holiness Pope Paul VI spoke of in his encyclical *Ecclasiam Suam*.

"For that matter, when you [Latin theologians] speak of ecclesiastical separation, you do not speak the same language as we Eastern Christians speak, consequently you are not understood by us. Easterners think of a separation from the Latin Church as nothing more than a separation from a particular local Church, according to their own conception of the matter.

"As for the primacy of the Roman Pontiff and its doctrinal formulation, although it had been declared many times in the earlier Western councils, it was not dogmatically defined [even in the West] until the First Vatican Council less than a hundred years ago. Until then it could not be considered, at least by the Orthodox, as anything except a canonical teaching. The council which restored Photius to office in 879 A.D. [as Ecumenical Patriarch] was content to draft a *modus vivendi* regulating the relations between the two Churches, without the theological implications that the West later drew from it in order to justify the doctrines of primacy and infallibility."

The True Foundation of Unity and Universality

The true foundation of the universality of the Church and its unity is the identity of the Redemptive Word with the Creative Word. As is also to be seen in the chapter on the concept of "mission", the Redemptive Word is also the Creative Word "by whom all things were made and without whom nothing that was created exists." (John 1, 3) But the Creative Word has planted in each human being a divine seed which the Greek Fathers call *sperma tou Logou*, or "seed of the Word." Through the centuries the Spirit of God has cultivated this seed in souls, preparing them, according to the "divine pedagogy," to receive the Word made flesh. The Church when preaching Christ to the most primitive people must utilize all that she finds in them, remembering that "God Himself is not far distant from those who seek the unknown God in shadows and images, for it is He who gives to all men life and breath and all things." (Acts 17: 25-28)

It is this identity of the Creative Word with the Redemptive Word which permits the Church of Christ to be universal, that is, to preach the Gospel to every man who comes into this world. It is this which also permits the Church to accomplish the unity of men by preaching as their common Brother the One who made them all out of nothing.

But in order that people may recognize in Christ the Word whose seed they carry within them, we must present the Christ found in the Gospel, from Bethlehem to Golgotha, not a Christ already "nationalized" by us, carrying our appearance and our uniform: a Christ imported from a Greek, Anglo-Saxon or Latin background, whom they can not assimilate. Christ can accomplish unity only to the extent that He is reborn in each country, in each generation, and in each people, so that each man can recognize Him as His own Brother, of His own family and race. Men want a Savior who is able to become their fellow citizen - a Christ conceived by the Holy Spirit without any Father except the Heavenly Father, so that they can both integrate Him and integrate into Him, the "First-born of all creatures." (Col. 1)

Christ must then accept peoples as they are because He made them this way. Vatican II said: "Since the kingdom of Christ is not of this world (cf. John 18:36), the Church or the people of God which prepares for the coming of this Kingdom takes nothing away from the temporal welfare of any people. On the contrary it fosters and takes to itself, insofar as they are good, the ability, riches and customs in which the genius of each people expresses itself. Taking them to itself it purifies, strengthens, elevates and ennobles them." (#13)

Indeed the Redemptive Word did not come to abolish the work of the Creative Word; He did not come to destroy His Creatures but to redeem them, to renew them and reconcile them by destroying their sins. There is a continuity in the action of God. God does not make a practice of destroying what He has previously accomplished. He only repairs and saves what man has been able to damage. The Word, having created man, also fashioned his spirit and his heart. Having directed through His seed the evolution of peoples through the centuries, He cannot deny what He has done. Christianity must then take on the entire man; it must take on peoples with their own genius, their language, their culture and even the forms of their worship. Furthermore, we must remember that Christ wants to save peoples by Himself becoming part of them. Just as He did not hesitate to cross the boundaries (culture, etc.) which separate men from each other.

The young Churches must participate actively in the building up of the Body of Christ. The Church must not only give to them, it must be nourished by them, enriched by their contribution. As the Conciliar document states: "Because of this catholicity each individual part contributes through its special gifts to the good of the other parts of the whole Church. Through the common sharing of gifts and through the common effort to attain fullness in unity, the whole Church and each of the parts receive increase. (#13)

"For the members of the people of God are called to hold their goods in common, and of each of the Churches the words of the Apostles apply: "According to the gift each has received, administer it to be one another as one stewards of the manifold grace of God. (I Peter 4:10)" (#13)

If the Church is content to have the world profit from a sole, local or national Christianity, then it will never reach maturity. Even though it might become a living and fervent Church in the process, it would not attain the fullness of Christ. In addition, It would not accomplish the unity of mankind, for in order to do that, men must *together* build up the Body of Christ on earth, according to the words of the Apostle.

Since Vatican II, the Catholic Church seems to have decided to open itself to this universality. The use of each peoples vernacular language in the predominantly Latin Liturgy is only a timid beginning. From now on the young Churches will celebrate in their own language an essentially Latin Mass, culturally foreign to them. The day must soon come that they will construct their own liturgy out of their own cultural and national mentalities and will pray their own prayers. But the prayer itself must be impregnated "with the faith and knowledge" of the Son of God. Each people must be able to reformulate its doctrine and express Jesus Christ, one of their own, as their spirit conceives Him again in the Holy Spirit and as the Holy Spirit reforms Him in their heart. The missionary must only fill the role of the Angel in the mystery of the Incarnation of the Word in the midst of the peoples, leaving to the new "people of God" the task of remaking their own Christ. As He came to Mary, "the Holy Spirit will come upon them and the Power of the Most High will overshadow" them. (Cf. Luke 1:35) Thus, He who is born in their midst will be *their* Son of Man, the only one capable of being their Savior.

Searching for Unity

It is an extraordinary phenomenon we are now witnessing. Nations, communities, Churches, and the whole material world itself are simultaneously engaging themselves in the effort to seek unity. This is gratifying because union is both God's will and can do nothing but benefit mankind both materially and spiritually.

37

A Voice from the Byzantine East

The time has passed when the civil and religious societies consider diversity incompatible with unity. Men of every race, of every color and religion, have begun to believe in the universal brotherhood of men and to renounce the separatist mentality and the fanatical sectarianism of the Middle Ages. Since the beginning of our own century international organizations have followed one another in the political, social and cultural fields. The two great wars, which serve as a test and did not bring about "a world safe for democracy" or a solution to any of the other problems dividing mankind, have shown that international conflicts cannot be settled by force. A new era of dialog has begun among peoples. And seeing that union between men, like union with God through love, generally cannot last unless accompanied by a certain salutary fear, God has permitted the threat of atomic to stop mankind at the very edge of the abyss into which it is almost thrown by war, each time that the dialog seemed to be ineffectual. As happens in every serious transition from one condition to another, the final victory of peaceful and fraternal coexistence is accomplished only in uncertainty and in the tempestuous times in which we live.

It is worth noting that at the same time that the human family was beginning a rebirth of fraternity amidst their distress, an unprecedented ecumenical movement emerged, seizing the Christian Churches. Formerly turned in upon themselves, hostile and intolerant toward one another, they are now setting out on a completely new path toward reconciliation marked by several distinguishing features, not the least of them being mutual respect, works of mercy done in unison and even common prayer for unity. It is not just by chance that both the world and the Church are simultaneously engaged in the search for unity. Since it was the Word Who made all things and Who guides the Church's destiny, isn't this same Word capable of presiding, and does He not actually preside, over the destiny of the whole world? "All men," the conciliar *Constitution on the Church* points out, "are called to this union with Christ, the light of the world, from whom we come, through whom we live and toward whom our whole life strains."(#3) And further: "the Church is in Christ like a sacrament or as a sign and instrument both of an intimate union with God and of the unity of the whole human race." It also shows us the connection between Christian unity and the present state of evolution in the human family when it says: "The present conditions of the world add greater urgency to this work of the Church so that all men, joined together more closely today by various social, technical and cultural ties, might also attain fuller unity with Christ." (#1)   the Spirit of Jesus Christ which directs the Church is exactly the same Spirit which leads all humanity toward its end: the building up of the Body of Christ (i.e. the Church).

The material world in all its diversity must also be involved in the search for unity. Created for man, it has a solidarity with him and shares his destiny. It has shared the curse that followed the sin of Adam ("Cursed be the soil because of you." - Genesis 3: 17-18); why then will it not be the object of redemption also, along with the body of man which is also material? "All creation is waiting," writes St. Paul to the Romans, "eager for the revelation of the sons of God: if it was made subject to emptiness [that is, man by his or God by His righteous vengeance].   Furthermore, it is hopeful of also being freed from the slavery of corruption in order to enter into the liberty of the glory of the children of God. Indeed we know that all creation up to now has groaned as if in childbirth." (Romans 8: 19-23)   How clearly the *Constitution* expresses this point: "The Church, to which we all are called in Christ Jesus ... will attain its full perfection only in the glory of heaven, when there will come the time of the restoration of all things (Acts 3:21). At that time the human race as well as the entire world, which is intimately related to man and attains to its end through him, will be perfectly re-established in Christ." (Cf. Ephesians 1: 10; Colossians 1: 20; 2 Peter 3: 10-13) (#48)

This idea, dear to the Bible, of the universe being "filled" by the creative presence of the Word leads us to believe, with St. Paul, that the Incarnation of the word and His Resurrection have placed the human nature at the head, not only of the whole human race, but also of all the created universe, for He was as concerned with its salvation as He had been at its fall. Thus we agree with the interpretation of the eminent scripture scholars at L'Ecole Biblique in Jerusalem regarding Paul's words to the Colossians: "God was pleased to make all the fullness dwell in Him [Jesus

Christ], and through Him, to reconcile all creation for Him."
(Col. 1: 19-20) The entire Epistle to the Ephesians further
develops this idea of Christ renewing the created world
which had been corrupted by sin and leading it back to God:
"He [God] has made us understand the mystery of His will,
His provident plan which He had formed in Christ in
advance, in order to accomplish it in the fullness of time: to
lead back under one Shepherd, Christ, all things, the heavenly beings as well as the earthly." (Eph. 1: 9-10)

Having said this, we do not consider it at all fanciful
to associate the material world, in all its immense variety,
with the work of human unity and Christian unity which
must be accomplished in the Church and by the Church. As
we have seen above, God has willed from the beginning of
this century to prepare a new era of universal brotherhood
for human society and for the Churches. From then on it
was entirely natural that God would at the same time open
the minds of men to the secrets of nature. They thus could
discover in it hidden resources suitable to facilitate the
physical communication between peoples as well as the dialog necessary to any reconciliation. And indeed there has
been an increase in discoveries, things now in operation and
still more on the planning boards, that were unknown and
not even dreamt of since the dawn of creation: steam, elec-
tricity, the airplane, radio, television, atomic power, even
space ships that have taken men to the moon and back, and
who would dare venture a guess about other events and discoveries the near future holds? We believe that exactly to
the extent that the human family renounces hate and the
meaning of war and destruction in order to draw closer the
bonds of universal brotherhood, God will place nature at
mankind's service so that participating in the work of
restoration it too might be the object of redemption and be
reconciled with God in Jesus Christ, it's Creator. Thus the
universe, in its immense variety and diversity, will be completely involved in the search for unity.

To emphasize further the precise connection
between the material world and the work of restoration
done by the Redemptive and Incarnate Word, it is necessary
to point out that nature did not begin to give its secrets to
man until after the Creative Word had been revealed to the
world in the Redemptive Word. In fact, the Apostle Paul

says to the Romans in chapter 8, verses 19 through 23: "Creation has been waiting ... subjected by man's sin to the slavery of corruption ... it was expecting deliverance from this slavery ... and has been groaning up till now as in childbirth."

"Cursed be the soil because of you" ..., for along with the earthy Paradise God locked up the riches and secrets of the material universe. The Redemptive Word alone, His coming and His victory over death, was able to reconcile humanity with God and thus break the chains which held men and the universe in captivity. Didn't the darkened sky and the shattered rocks manifest the part taken by the material world not share in the victory of Christ over death? "Already the final age of the world has come upon us (cf. I Cor. 10: 11), and the restoration of the world is irrevocably decreed." (#48)

On the other hand, the material world, enclosing the riches deposited there by the Creative word, could not reveal itself to man until the Word had revealed Himself first. "The first-born of all creation, it is in Him that all things in heaven and on earth were created ... The first-born from the dead, it was necessary that Christ attain primacy in everything." (Col. I: 15-19) It was necessary that Christ come and that He rise unto glory, in order to give men, reconciled with God by the Cross, access to the natural mysteries hidden till then in the material universe. Hundreds, thousands and perhaps millions of years have passed since creation, and man, no less intelligent or curios than today, remained an outsider in this locked temple, whose keys were held by the Son, the only heir. But "the Word was made flesh and dwelt among us and we saw His glory." (John 1: 14) And "He who sits upon the throne declared, 'Behold, I am making all things new.'" (Rev. 21: 5) Since it has been freed from its chains, the new universe was in a position to free its secrets to the new man, made new by the coming of its father and brother in the person of Jesus Christ. But it was necessary that the Risen Christ, first-born in the order of creation as well as in the order of re-creation, come into contact with a dispersed and scattered humanity and manifest His glory throughout all the inhabited earth. It took almost two thousand years for Christ to be preached to the entire world and for men to hear again the words addressed by God to our first parents:

"Fill the earth and subdue it." (Gen. 1: 28) And thus we are contemporaries of Jesus in the conquest of the earth and of space. We are really His contemporaries, for what is a mere two thousand years in the succession of centuries which have passed since creation and which will pass until the end of time? When the world will reach its end, the tens of centuries which preceded and followed the Incarnation of the Word will appear as a single day at the peak of all time, or rather as the rose-colored dawn of a new day when people, reconciled with God in Jesus Christ, will have begun to become reconciled among themselves, involved in the search for the reconciliation of the material universe itself which previously, due to man's sin, was involved in the conflict between men.

Henceforth mankind seems to want to reconstruct the Body of Christ in brotherhood and unity while, at the same time, building a new world.

We close this chapter with an appropriate quotation from the *Constitution on the Church*: "The Church both prays and labors so that the entire world may truly become the People of God, the Body of the Lord and the Temple of the Holy Spirit, that in Christ, the Head of all, all glory and honor may be given to the Creator and Father of the universe." (#17)

Notes

1. Constitution on the Church, #50. All further references to this document of the Second Vatican Council will be by paragraph number only.

2. The concept of the Mystical Body of Christ, revived in the Western Church by Pope Pius XII's Encyclical *Mystici Corporis*, was prevalent in the early Church Fathers' writings and has always been taught by the Eastern Churches.

3. Cf. Chapter Nine, "Uniatism and Ecumenism".

4. This is discussed at length in other parts of this book. [R.B.]

5. Most of the administrative details were handled by a group of local clergy. Later this was to develop into the college of Cardinals whose members residing in Rome evolved into the Curia.

6. Thus the following statement of Bishop Kallistos of Dioklea (Timothy Ware), in *Diakonia* (1885-6). "The *filioque* controversy which has separated us for so many centuries is more than a mere technicality, but it is not insoluble. Qualifying the firm position taken when I wrote *The Orthodox Church* twenty years ago, I now believe, after further study, that the problem is more in the area of semantics than in any basic doctrinal differences." [F.S.]

Part II - The Eastern Churches

Three - Understanding the Eastern Churches

Roman Catholics now seem to manifest more good-will toward their Eastern Catholic brethren and we rejoice in this. However, we must also point out that their new attitude is one of condescension, pity and sympathy and they really have no idea that we Easterners possess the *better* part of Christian tradition rather than the lesser part of it. To back up that strong statement, we have but to remember the fact that precious few Western prelates attended the first councils of the Church: Councils defining the Holy Trinity, the Divinity of Christ, the Natures of Christ, the Divine Motherhood of Mary, and so on. These doctrines form the foundation of true Christianity!

Another perspective on the same theme is seen in a quotation of the Byzantine theological writer K.J. Mortimer, born in England and now teaching in the Middle East: "The Byzantine rite is by far the richest and most splendid of all rites. This is not to be wondered at, for this was the imperial rite of the one great stable civilization whose whole life was penetrated by a consciousness of Christian revelation and of Christ's empire throughout the entire universe. For eleven hundred years the city on the Golden Horne was the greatest on earth with its incomparable riches, with the great Church of the Holy Wisdom and its realms of scintillating mosaics and ikonography, with the Studion monastery filled with a thousand monks. And yet, at the same time as the Empire grew richer, the monasteries and the whole concept of monasticism flourished. There can be no inventory taken of the innumerable treasures the emperors and tsars showered on Mount Athos, whose monks were once counted in tens of thousands!"

Speaking about the liturgy, Mortimer says: "Byzantium incorporated into its liturgy the science and poetry and prayer of the most brilliant and widely-cultured Fathers of the Church, and took into its own art the dream world of the Cappadocian wilderness where persecuted Christians, having left everything, retreated so that they could keep the faith pure. It was also in that strange country that they caught a glimpse of the supernatural which has been perpetuated ever since in the theology of holy ikons. How sad it is that we who are accustomed to a secularized world can no longer conceive of a civilization whose whole structure (life, art, politics, science, etc.) is a living expression of a common intuition of the Holy Wisdom!"

Three general observations on the way Roman Catholics view Eastern Catholics are in order here. The ideas here are basically the same ones presented to the Fathers at the Second Vatican Council for, taken as a whole, the thinking of these bishops was just as deficient as that of their flocks. The observations fall into three categories: theological, historical and practical.

First: What is said in the first sentence of the prologue to the Second Vatican Council's Decree on the Eastern Catholic Churches shows that the notion of the Catholic Church is still very inadequate. I quote it: "The Catholic Church holds in high esteem the institutions of the Eastern Churches, their liturgical rites, ecclesiastical traditions, and Christian way of life." These are the very first words of that document and it is surprising that after so much work on the nature of the Church in the Council the theologians still did not clarify this erroneous notion.

The universal Church is, in fact, composed of all the particular local Churches united by the Holy Spirit and structured, since the first centuries, around the great sees of Christendom. The most efficient and the principal of these sees was in Rome, and was so with the consent of all by reason of the apostolic succession of the See of Peter. But this universal Church must not be confused with that "universality" of the Western and Latin Church which began to exist as such only later, notably in the time to Charlemagne. Little by little, and due to the canonical separation between East and West, the latter one day found itself all alone, having lost respect for the ancient patriarchal structure of the Church which the first centuries had sanctioned and which it (the West) has attempted to suffocate. One way the West lost its idea of the patriarchal system of ecclesiastical government was the creation of artificial or titular patriarchates. This was done during the time of the

Crusades when the Roman Pontiffs installed Latin prelates in the Eastern Patriarchal Sees and removed the true patriarchs who were the legitimate pastors of their people.

Moreover, in the centuries following down till today Latin missionaries, hardly better inspired than in earlier days, have set up Latin Churches in the East, whence have arisen rivalries unfavorable to the Eastern Churches. It is also true that certain parts of the Eastern Churches that united with Rome have, over the course of the centuries, been aggregated to the Western structure. As for the "separated" Eastern Christians, they have always preserved the initial conception realizing in practice that which Pope Paul VI wrote in his Encyclical *Ecclesiam Suam*; whereas Westerners, on the contrary, have held almost exclusively to the second formula.

When we speak of ecclesiastical separation we simply do not speak the same language and therefore do not understand one another. Easterners consider a separation from the Latin Church as a break with a *particular* Church. Westerners think of it as a separation from the *universal* Church for this is *their* conception of schism. Now, the *Decree on the Eastern Catholic Churches* is entirely conceived in the latter manner, as if the Catholic Eastern Churches were parts or appendices of the "universal" Latin Church; this theory cannot logically be admitted. How unfortunate it is that the Council's *Decree on the Eastern Catholic Churches* was not entirely recast and rewritten in more realistic terms for, as it stands, its presents a false perspective to the world.

Second: The doctrinal formulation of the primacy of the Roman Pontiff, although spoken of several times in previous western Councils, was dogmatically defined only at Vatican I. Until then it could be considered (at least by the Orthodox) as only a canonical doctrine or "theologumenon". The undivided Church certainly saw the Roman Pontiff as the first Bishop of the Church enjoying unbreakable rights such as presiding at Ecumenical Councils (or at least to watch over their conduct and to sign their decrees). The Easterners had appealed to him in serious matters but this recourse was interpreted as being more canonical than dogmatic in implication.

If, then, the two Churches were not theologically in opposition on the doctrine of the primacy and if, by the formula of the *filioque*, the Eastern theology of the procession of the Holy Spirit was not denied (as was confirmed at the Unity Council at Florence), we can declare that the Churches of both East and West - even after the schism - were not as separated as is commonly believed and that they both have preserved their communion in the faith.

As for the conflict, that was between two particular and local Churches or between the Eastern Patriarchs and the Roman Pontiffs who wanted to extend to the Orient the same type of power they possess over the Occident. Never conscious of having been separated from the Church, the Easterns felt that they themselves, together with the Latin Church (and at least in the same manner as the West) were - and *are* - the Church. History shows us that they constituted the most important part of Christianity and had, by themselves, defined the truths of our Faith and had given the Church its best theologians who made up 98% of the Fathers of the first ecumenical councils.

At the First Vatican Council a century ago, when there was talk of defining the primacy of Roman Pontiff and of thus determining the theological structure of the Church, all the Fathers present were Latin except for a tiny handful of bishops. The definition they published, we must bear in mind, was very important to Eastern Christians, in fact it was probably more important for the Easterns than for the Latins because it affected the ecclesiastical structure of the Eastern Christians even more than the West.

Third: A brief mention of *communicatio in sacris*, that is, participation in sacraments, prayers and services with non-Catholics (in this case, we are referring to the exchanging of sacraments between Catholics and Orthodox) is in order here. The reviving of *communicatio in sacris* between Catholics and Orthodox (particularly the statement made by the Russian Orthodox Church in December of 1969)[1] is encouraging because this was the normal practice of almost all Eastern Catholic groups[2] for many years. Sharing the sacraments with Orthodox Christians was common pastoral usage in many regions of the world and ceased only at the beginning of the nineteenth century (except among some Melkites) by an awkward application of the post-Tridentine decrees in the West. These laws indicated that since Protestants are heretics their Eucharist could not be considered valid, therefore no Catholic was allowed to participate in Eucharistic services or to receive Communion in their churches. By some quirk the same idea (i.e. no *communicatio in sacris*) was later extended to Orthodoxy[3] even though Orthodox sacraments have never been pronounced invalid.

In this same vein, the philosopher-theologian Vladimir Soloviev (1853-1900) called "the Russian Newman," believed in intercommunion, too. He held that the two great traditional Churches of East and West were never separated *de jure*, an historical fact not widely publicized until *circa* 1950. This is why he did not conceive of "his reception [in 1896] of Holy Communion from [Byzantine rite Roman Catholic Father Nicholas] Tolstoy as a sign of formal conversion: if the two Churches are not separated, intercommunion is implicitly allowed. [His reception of the Eucharist from Father Nicholas was merely] the formal recognition of the primacy of the Roman See, which he had recognized ever since he wrote *Russia and the Universal Church* [in the late 1880s]. Rebaptism and reconfirmation were consequently not only unnecessary but impossible [according to canon law of both Catholicism and Orthodoxy. As a result, he] disapproved of individual conversions which occurred within the circle."[4]

When a non-Catholic Christian finds it necessary to join the Catholic Church, I am of the opinion that he should adhere strictly to his previous rite as much as possible. With Protestants, they should enter the Roman rite and try to become comfortable in it, for it is their Church of origin and, though they may be forced to make some minor adjustments, this is really the place where they belong and where they should, sooner or later, begin to feel at home. When speaking of Eastern Christians one will observe that there are many Eastern rites within the pale of Catholicism in which any Easterner can find a Church corresponding to the Church he left and there he can feel at home. Now in exceptional cases a special synodal commission or even the Holy See of Rome could serve as arbiter and judge until a satisfactory and just conclusion were reached. In this, I am in full accord with the Conciliar *Decree on the Eastern Catholic Churches* promulgated by Vatican Council II, as well as the great majority of the clergy and faithful of the Eastern Catholic Churches.

Wisdom is a requisite for all serving in the cause of unity between Orthodoxy and Catholicism because the feelings of Eastern Christians must be taken into full consideration and not dismissed lightly. So let us be wise but let us also be fair and, above all, lovingly tolerant of those Easterners who do not see eye-to-eye with the Western ways of doing things. Let us not judge the quarrels and schisms of past times with the mentality of our Latin ancestors in the faith, but with our own. We live, thanks be to God, in a century of openness and liberty, even *religious* liberty (as is evidenced by the Second Vatican Council's *Declaration on Religious Liberty*)! We realize that within the bosom of the same Church we can have members who think and express themselves differently. Such liberty was not always tolerated in the past and in certain historical periods was even banned. History also demonstrates that the Church has often become divided just to defend certain formulae. Instead of trying to reconcile their differences with the truth, particular churchmen imposed their own local or even personal formulae upon the entire Church. Such actions have done untold damage to the unity of Christendom.

If we were to utilize the methods of yesterday, e.g. if we had at the head of the Second Vatican Council a Cardinal Humbert capable of issuing a bull of excommunication in a single moment of anger (in the name of a Pope dead for three months), how many of the authentic Catholic bishops who participated it that Council would have walked out excommunicated, at the risk of discovering many years later that the formulae they had espoused were not contradictory and were entirely valid?[5]

Let us forever rejoice that God has given us a better age in which to have been born, and let us thank Him by diligently working to repair the Mystical Body of Christ by restoring to it all the broken parts.

Notes

1. The statement allows Russian Orthodox priests to give the Eucharist to any Catholics who desire it. The Vatican had already given permission for its priests to do the same.

2. Melkites in the Near East were the only group that continued any *communicatio in sacris* with the Orthodox despite Rome's repeated orders to the contrary.

3. As closely as we have been able to determine, this was the deed of a handful of ill-informed Latin missionaries working in the Middle East.

4. Egbert Munzer, *Soloviev: Prophet of Russian-Western Unity* (London: Hollis and Carter, 1956, p. 93.)

5. For example, they could have later found out that the primacy was not at odds with collegiality, or that the so-called Monophysite theory and the Eastern Orthodox doctrine of the procession of the Holy Spirit could also be true.

Four - One Church, East and West

If after ten centuries of schism and of separate development the Latin and Eastern Churches still find that they are substantially alike, may we dare to think that a thousand years ago they had reasons of great importance that caused them to separate? Certainly not! The schism would not have taken place if the Churches of the West and the East were not indirectly involved in the conflict which set the two empires in opposition to one another. There are, I believe, times unfavorable to dialogue and times which are favorable. The Eastern Schism, for which a more appropriate name might be the Great Christian Schism (for the responsibility is shared by both sides), took place at a time when the Christian East and West could not enter into a productive dialogue on a basis of equality.

The minor clashes between the Latin and Eastern Churches, which up to this time had been regarded as trifling incidents between brothers of the same family, took on more and more the disturbing proportions of the great conflict which set the two empires at loggerheads. The Latin Church began to see in this development a resistance to the primatial authority of Peter, and the Orthodox saw it an attempt to dominate which appeared contrary to the principle of the primacy of service.

The primacy of the Bishop of Rome, which the tradition of a thousand years had consecrated as a body of unity, began to be thought of (in the East) as the extension of the authority of one local Church over the Church universal. This was the start of the crisis that made its first appearance around the fifth century and ended with the separation.

Some modern Catholic historians, men of outstanding merit, interpret the Great Schism as the checkmate of efforts aimed at applying Roman centralization to the Churches of the East, which during ten centuries of union with Rome had become accustomed to combining unity with legitimate diversity.

The Churches of the East, in fact, opposed centralization from the very beginning and opposed it strenuously. Why? Some say due to loyalty to the civil powers. Maybe it was because of pride, others say. The Easterners think differently. The Eastern Churches had practiced a systems of collegial synods in Church government during the first thousand years and the eye of Rome, ever watching discipline, practice and doctrine of all the Christian Churches especially those in union with her, never found anything abnormal in this system. Furthermore, the ecclesiastical authorities of the East found no justification for the new change in the authentic tradition shared by both Churches. Then too, the Eastern Churches, founded by the Apostles or their immediate successors and not owing either their birth or development to the Western Church, found that they possessed a religious, theological, liturgical, monastic and disciplinary heritage different from that of the West, yet not opposed to it. Now it is evident that it does not take long for a Church governed by groups which are strangers to its own tradition to find its own tradition substantially diminished.

So it was understandable that Roman centralization seemed to the Easterners to be a means of imposing uniformity, a move which could cast doubt on the legitimacy of their own religious heritage. Yet this was a religious heritage which they had received from their forefathers through an apostolic succession whose credentials were impeccable.

What was needed then, was a dialogue to make clear the nature of the mystery of the Church, the relation between the primacy and collegiality, between the local Diocese of Rome and the primatial power of the Bishop of Rome. But this interchanging of opinions could not maturely take place either in the eleventh century or at the Council of Florence in the fifteenth because the unfavorable social and political framework of those times made it impossible.

One might ask why God did not intervene as He intervenes to prevent all doctrinal error in the Church. The answer is not difficult. In the first place, Christian unity should not be exclusively the work of God, but the work of men as well. But it is also true that since the purpose of the primacy of Peter is to protect the integrity of the Christian heritage, God would not want this same primacy to be exercised in such a way that this integrity would suffer harm. The two main authentic and apostolic traditions, though complementary, are different; i.e. the Latin tradition and the Eastern are in fact the two halves of the Christian heritage, and taken together make up that total and integral Christianity which, as a whole, inherits the promise of Divine protection to the end of time. Any unity which would be made in such a way that either of the apostolic traditions suffered harm would impoverish the Church instead of enriching it.

The Catholic unity towards which ecumenism is moving will be much more comprehensive and fruitful than the ecumenism of the present. The Catholic unity we know today manifests itself as something partial and more Latin than anything else. It groups together the original Latin Churches of the West and the Latin Churches founded by them in mission countries, along with the modest little communities of Uniate Eastern Churches, most of which are substantially Latinized even though they have kept somewhat their external liturgical rites. Today only Orthodoxy possesses the authentic Eastern tradition, though at times in a diminished form; only the union of Latins and Orthodox on the level of equality can bring together the apostolic tradition in its fullness and make Catholic unity complete.

I speak of unity based on equality because on the day that union will come about, Orthodoxy will have at least as much to give as to receive. It must, therefore, share equally in the government of the reunited Church, just as must the Latin Church, under the primacy of Peter, of course.

Actually, the schism has mutilated both Churches. The Western Church, when it lost communion with the Apostolic Sees of the East, lost the most collegial segment of the episcopal college. Centralization progressed at an extraordinary pace without anyone being able to hold it in check. The Western Church has been governed by the Roman Curia, and for all practical purposes, by the *congresso* or weekly meeting of the officials of the Curia. By this procedure, the Curia members who reside elsewhere are reduced, in actual practice, to *titular* members without a vote, simply because it is physically impossible for them to attend the weekly *congresso* in Rome.

On the other side, the Eastern Churches have lost, through the Great Schism, communion with the center of unity of the whole Catholic Church which is the Bishop of

Old Rome. Excessive decentralization has weakened them considerably, making difficult the regular practice of episcopal collegiality, which nevertheless remains their principal system of government.

But God who extracts good from evil has permitted this unhappy schism to occur in order to protect the Orthodox Churches from centralization and Latinization, thus rendering ecumenical dialogue immensely profitable and giving promise of great enrichment for the Church when it is again made one.

This dialogue on an equal basis between Latins and Orthodox, which was practically impossible at the time of the Schism, is becoming a reality today, as it rightfully should be, for if even hostile nations are utilizing all types of international bodies to help bring themselves together in the pursuit of peace, should the Churches at least not do likewise?

This East-West Christian dialogue should be accompanied by an even greater effort at decentralization which was begun at the Second Vatican Council, and in the Orthodox Churches it should accompany an effort of extremely qualified centralization around Peter's successor and in the framework of traditional collegiality.

In this dialogue, which primarily concerns the Latin and Orthodox Churches, the Eastern Uniates will have a role as witnesses which, though secondary, is nevertheless necessary. In de-latinizing themselves, they must come at last to live more fully in accordance with traditional Eastern forms, customs and practices, while remaining within the heart of Catholicism, in order to make Latin Catholics more familiar with these forms and make the dialogue easier and more effective. Indeed, as is mentioned in the chapter on Uniatism and ecumenism, this is the only way the Eastern Catholic Uniates can be of any real use to the Church of Jesus Christ until it is fully united.

Five - The Two Christian Traditions

The problem of Christian unity is different for the Orthodox and for Protestants because their respective relationships with the Latin Church are essentially different. The Protestant Churches detached themselves from the Latin Church, their mother, in the bosom of which they were born and of which they constituted an integral part. The Eastern Churches have always recognized the Primacy of the Bishop of Rome, although that recognition must be considered as a rather vague one, even though they were never part of the Latin Church. As sister Churches of the Latin Church, they do not emanate from the Western-Latin Church. They owe the Latin Church neither their existence, their substance, nor their dogmatic and disciplinary development. The Eastern Churches, and consequently the Orthodox Church, are historically *source* Churches just as the Latin Church is in the West.

Founded by the Apostles and their immediate disciples, these Churches were born without the aid of any other Church since they were in existence *before* others. Their discipline and liturgy came into being without the assistance of the West, since their discipline and liturgies are distinctively different from those of the West. Even their doctrine, substantially identical with that of the West, is differently assimilated and differently lived. Notice that the books authored by the Fathers of the Greek Church are highly esteemed and are place side by side with those of the Latin Fathers without, however, being confused with them; two geniuses, two different but valid Christian inspirations, both traced back to Christ, the living source, but whose waters have passed through lands of different natures, through civilizations and mentalities that are quite varied and possessing properties that are, today, very different and often irreducible. It is vital that we do not forget this so that we may not make the mistake of reducing the fact of the separation to a mere rash impulse, in order that we may correctly evaluate and accurately measure the possibilities of and methods to obtain a reunion.

To further illustrate this will suffice to briefly show how the same Christian mysteries (including the sacraments, etc.) and the same feasts are envisaged, understood and lived differently by the Eastern and Western Churches. For example, let us consider the dogma of the Most Holy Trinity. Our Eastern theology has remained faithful to the doctrinal presentation of the Fathers elaborated at the time of the Ecumenical Councils, notably Nicaea I and Constantinople I. On the subject of circumincession of the Divine Persons, our Church has not permitted itself to become influenced by the Western theses of Augustinian theology which were spread throughout the West during the middle ages and are still popular in most Latin theological circles. In like manner, the East always insists not exclusively upon the doctrine of the so-called Christological Councils but also upon the theological dimensions that the Fathers contemporary to those Councils have given it. This is particularly noteworthy on the subject of the Incarnation of the Divine Word, conceived especially as a divinization of human nature by Christ. "God became man so that man (i.e. humankind) may become gods," or god-like, as St. Athanasius of Alexandria said. Or, to be more specific, He became man so that men might be able to receive God's grace and become divine. And yet again in different words; "... so that man may become by grace, that which God is by nature." This doctrine has been almost exclusively blurred out and even concealed, as it were, from the Western Christian faithful by the propagation of the Latin doctrinal theory of vicarious satisfaction.

These different way of understanding and assimilating the same dogmas have influenced both the liturgy and the feasts of the respective Churches. The Eastern Catholic liturgies and feasts, which are identical with those of the Orthodox, manifest this contention. Let us take Christmas as an example.

The feast of Christ's Nativity, just as the feast of the Epiphany, in the East celebrates this divinization of human nature. It is not the same in the Latin Church. In passing I would also like to mention the feast of the Annunciation which with both the Eastern Christian Uniates and

Orthodox commemorates the most solemn and the most spectacular event in human history - the Incarnation of the very Word of God in the womb of the Virgin; while, in contrast, the focus of this same feast in the Latin Church is upon the glories of the Virgin chosen by God to be the Mother of His Son.

By these examples, cited at random, we see that there is in Christianity from the very beginning, two main currents which channel the riches of the Redemption in two parallel directions which can reciprocally complete and enrich one another without merging. As long as East is East and West is West there will always be, as there always was, two Churches in One. With God's help they can unite but not fuse, co-exist in unity but never in uniformity. Each of the two Churches will necessarily keep its own character, physiognomy and personality. Our Lord said to His followers; "Be one, as my Father and I are One." Now, the Trinity, united in the same Nature, the Father, the Son and the Holy Spirit each keeps His own distinct Personality; *one* God in *three* persons. It is in the same manner that Christ wants to see Christian unity realized: two Churches remaining distinct but consubstantially one in the universal Church, which is truly one in its supernature, in its hierarchical society.

Insisting on the collegial power of the Apostles the Orthodox Churches are evolving toward a greater and greater autonomy, while the Catholic Church during the course of the last few centuries has moved in the opposite direction, toward that of centralization. Catholics and Orthodox will be able to unite only by balancing one another in a mutual harmony, a tendency which finally seems to be catching on in the Latin Church today.

In this discussion, I have set the Orthodox Church and the Latin Church in opposing camps, however, the question of unity is a problem between Orthodox and Catholics. Why? Because the Catholic Church is in fact, even in this modern era (despite most of its liturgical changes - and admittedly some of them are quite odd), quite Latin in the overwhelming majority, as the Church (or Churches) of the East are Orthodox in the very great majority.

This was evident in the Second Vatican Council where the Eastern Bishops numbering 130 were lost in an assembly of more than two thousand Fathers, and the Patriarchs of the East from the great Apostolic Sees in the East found themselves, in the person of the Eastern Catholic Patriarchs, drowned in this overwhelming assembly and almost disappeared behind the sacred purple and red of the hundred cardinals who did not even exist in the early Church.

The Church has evolved, some will say. That is true, but it has evolved only on one side without taking account of those who, *by the very will of Christ*, are called to be one-half of it! For our brothers, the Orthodox hierarchs, to admit straight off our factual evolution is to all at once renounce what they are and to dissolve their Churches into the Latinism that today continues to characterize the Catholic Church universal. Our Eastern Catholics continually remind Rome - and we are now just beginning to see the fruits of these labors - that union is made to enrich everyone and not to impoverish anyone.

When I saw today's Catholic Church, united in the Second Vatican Council blessed by God, it appeared to thirst for the day when Orthodoxy, with its 250 million faithful, will be represented in it in proportion to the patrimony which its illustrious Fathers, great Doctors and holy monks have bequeathed to Christianity and with which they did not cease to enrich and nourish the Churches of the East and West.

Some wanted to say that the Council was not a Council of union. I will agree, but so long as Christians are divided, no Council enlivened with the Spirit of Jesus Christ can be disinterested in union, as the participants in Vatican II proved. They seemed to want to serve the cause of union in a great way. In fact, they made numerous strides in that direction which are history today.

As for the future, I foresee that when the newer Christian communities everywhere (including the old Christian communities of the West who have received Baptism from the Roman Church, their mistress and mother) will have soon found their native tongue in their worship and even perhaps their own national rites, when they will have found in their regional and national synods the climate favorable to their free and unhindered expansion - then the Catholic Church, adequately decentralized and generous to its children and trusting in those who have received Baptism from its own hands, will have cleared the first obstacle on the path toward union with those who have received the same Baptism from Eastern and Greek apostolic hands.

Part III - Uniting East and West

Six - In Pursuit of Orthodox-Catholic Unity

More people are interested in Christian unity than ever before, but I wonder how many of them genuinely understand what unity means and what it really entails.

If you ask a Christian, even a well-informed one, he would probably say: "We will have unity when the leaders of the two Churches reach agreement." We would admit that, at first glance, this is reasonable, but I suggest that we examine the statement more closely.

With regard to Orthodox-Catholic unity, we have received the impression that union would be achieved if the leaders of the Orthodox Churches would come to terms with the Roman Pontiff, e.g.. on the infallibility and primacy of the Pope. (The other minor differences, most of which reduce themselves to problems semantics, would fall into place once the above issues are resolved.)

I contend that to make Christian unity an agreement between the heads of the Churches and to consider the higher clergy as chief, and indeed only, agents of this union would be wrong. It would have the effect of reducing the Church of Christ to the level of a mere human society - a type of society where, as history has shown, the whims of a handful often decide the future of nations. In other words, this theory debases the mystery of the Passion and Redemption, which the Lord Himself offered as a magnificent prayer for unity, making it a mere *business* contract between men alone.

Furthermore, I contend that Christian unity should not be regarded as a compromise between the parties, with success depending exclusively upon the skills of a minority who happen to be entrusted with the government of Christ's Church. It should be considered the task of *all* Christians, for *all* are incorporated into Christ in some way or another, and *all* look to Him for their salvation.

Nevertheless, we must admit that a great deal of our present-day efforts toward unity are still being directed toward the visible union of all men in the One Church. I would be the last to deny that this was one of Our Savior's objectives but I would strongly disagree with those who feel that visible union was His only objective.[1] His central goal was to win men's hearts and only then to obtain their loyalty to His Church, the next logical step.

Practically everyone is convinced that if the leaders of the Orthodox world could sit down and reach agreement with the Roman Pontiff now, the union of both Churches would be instantaneous for, in these days, Christian unity seems dependent exclusively upon our ecclesiastical leaders.[2] But to view the Church as a kind of bicameral body with the laity occupying the lower house is to exaggerate the clergy's role out of proportion.

Orthodoxy, faithful to the tradition of the early Church, has a slightly different outlook reflected in the term, the People of God (in Greek: *laos theou*). Our own word "laity" is derived from it. However, whenever Orthodoxy uses the term she means both the people and the clergy *together*. In her connotation of the word the clergy becomes necessary part of the People of God, an integral part of the laity, and not a class set apart from the majority. Restoration of this concept, and all that it implies, to the modern Catholic Church would contribute to the noble cause of unity for it would assist our Church in becoming more like Orthodoxy, more democratic, and more like the early Christian Church.

Prior to attempting true unity, however, we must arrive at an even greater degree of maturity and perfection[3] than we have today. There is still too much indifference to our cause and even open opposition brought about by the closing of oneself to the divine loving graces, and the outright rejection of God's graces *above all* delays the advent of that glorious day of reunion.

Notes

1. To restore a proper balance in one's thinking, those who feel this was Christ's only purpose should, but only to a limited extent, emulate the modern Christian (Protestant) fundamentalist. The latter seeks inner union with God to

such a great extent that he frequently sees no need for a visible structured Church. If it is there, it is convenient. If it is not there, it doesn't really matter anyway.

2. Those of us who still think that the "business-contract-between-the-leaders" type of union is perfectly acceptable should remember that twice before we had this artificial brand of unity. It failed both times. As any material on the Catholic Council of Lyons and the Council of Florence will attest, the higher clergy and diplomats were prepared for the union but the people were not.

3. See the first chapter in this book, entitled "Christian Unity and the Salvation of the World" for elaboration.

Seven - Equality: the Basis of Union Between Orthodoxy and Catholicism

In this chapter we shall discuss a few general considerations which we feel the Church must deal with if it truly wishes to effectively contribute to Christian unity. We believe that union can be reached if we define unity as "a union of Churches in which Latins and Orthodox share true equality, as they did before the schism, and as they must share today, in all justice and in truth."

The Eastern Churches are not fringe-Churches. Together with the Latin Church, they are themselves the Church, and are on an equal footing with it. They possess half of the Christian heritage, and not the lesser half by any means! The Catholic Church ought not to base its relations with the Eastern Churches on charity, but on justice and truth. Therefore, the Roman Catholic Church must avoid treating the Eastern Churches with that type of kindness sometimes dealt out to beggars and criminals.

There is no particular reason for merely admiring the Eastern Churches nor is there cause for showing them compassion in any official document.[1] One can find just as many objects for admiration and compassion in the Latin Church. Moreover, to show them any particular solitude in a Church or Conciliar document is tantamount to identifying the Western Church with *the* Church, i.e. the Church Universal. We regret to say that this is exactly what happened at Vatican II. *Orientalium Ecclesiarum* strongly implied that the Eastern Catholic Churches are *outside* "the Church", since one cannot be both the subject and the object, whether of admiration or compassion, at the same time (not unless you divide the Church of Christ into two classes - one the privileged protection class, and the other under its tutelage). Incredible? Yes, but this really happened! The only valid conclusion is that the Eastern Catholic Churches have suffered great harm by the promulgation of that document!

It was our fear that this would happen. Consequently, we asked the Second Vatican Council not to produce any special conciliar papers on the Eastern Churches alone when such matter pertained to the entire Church.

We were saying that the Council must not present the Eastern Churches as some sort of "private" Churches unless, by the same token, she would willingly admit that the Latin Church is just as much of a "private" Church. Also, we urged that the Patriarchal institution must not be made to appear as a local and exclusively Eastern phenomenon. It must be brought out that the See of Rome itself is diocesan, patriarchal and primatial *all at once*, and that the Ecumenical Councils and tradition never isolated it from the Patriarchal Sees of the East. Conversely, the Catholic Church must not reserve to the See of Rome the titles Apostolic See or Holy See, titles to which the Apostolic Sees of the East have just as much right! Nor must the title "Vicar of Christ" be reserved to the Bishop of Rome, for every validly consecrated bishop is a Vicar of Jesus Christ.

Bishops Should Govern Their Own Churches

All of the Churches ought to be governed by their own bishops; Eastern Christians have never conceived of Church government in any other way. Now if the Catholic Church insists on the primacy of the bishop of Rome to the exclusion of his titles as Bishop and Patriarch, it threatens to make the universal Church a mere extension of the RoMan-Latin Church. The pope and his colleagues *must not be entrusted habitually and normally* with the government of all the Churches. This would be particularly out of place for the Orthodox Churches, accustomed as they are through a tradition two thousand years old to a hierarchical Church government which is capable of tempering its exercise and keeping it from pratically eliminating the College of Bishops. The direct power that the Latin Church attributes to the pope "over" the bishops, clergy and faithful of the Church does not make him the ruling bishop of every diocese. The pope does not govern all the Churches *aequali modo*. He cannot excercise, normally or habitually, in all the dioceses the role he excecises in Rome as its bishop. Nor can he exercise, normally and habitually, in the Eastern Patriarchates the role he exercises in the Latin Church in his capacity as Patriarch of the West.

It must be grasped once and for all that if each Church wants and ought to be governed from within, without detriment to the primacy of the successors of Peter in Rome, this desire does not spring from any spirit of nationalism or chauvinism. Rather it is for the greater good of the whole Christendom. If a Church is ruled, directly or indirectly, by men who are strangers to its religious, national or social traditions, it will eventually end up being stripped of these traditions and will become a foreign Church in her own country.

The history of Uniatism provides us with some obvious examples of this process. The Church is catholic (i.e., universal) only inasmuch as it adapts itself to different peoples and takes on their physiognomy.

In order to be catholic and universal the Church, as we have seen, must not impose on other peoples the civilization and traditions of only one particular region, nation or continent. The Church is to take in and assimilate as much, if not more, as it is to give out. This is how it will Christianize all civilizations and all human values.

Uniformity *versus* **Universality**

The catholicity of the Church does not rest upon the fact that it imposes upon men of all countries and races a certain uniformity in Church custom, in ways of prayer, or in the interpreting of the living the Gospel. Rather its catholicity resides in its capacity to adapt to all peoples, in all periods of history. Yet there is something else: Christ (and all the Apostles and Fathers) passed down to us an immense and varied Christian heritage to which the various civilizations and great personalities have brought their own spiritual riches. There is an Eastern face of Christianity as there is a Western one, just as there are both a Greek and Latin Patrology. They are not contradictory but complementary, and together they constitute the integral Christian tradition. the modern Church must become

Catholic not so much in the number and diversity of its children but in the integrity of its Christian patrimony. It professes this in theory, and it must *now* put the theory into practice. A Church which would be exclusively Latin and Western (or, for that matter, exclusively Eastern) in its thought, its spirituality, and its organization, dare not claim to be Catholic. Why? Because she would not possess the *universal* Christian heritage. The fact that it may admit different liturgical forms is scant argument, since liturgy or "rite" is one thing and "Church" is another.

The Church will be universal only when it includes *as equal* the two major authentic and apostolic traditions - Latin and Orthodox. Likewise a Council is ecumenical only when it draws its inspiration from *both* traditions.

It was according to this line of thinking that the Orthodox Churches accepted dialogue, an exchange of views *between equals*. If the Roman Catholic Church does not want to create more obstacles or to compromise the cause of unity, it must free itself of any and all tutelage. Would that the entire Church might pattern itself on the spirit behind the first meeting of Pope Paul VI and Patriarch Athenagoras I, for this is the only valid pattern for the great encounter of the Christian East and Christian West.

Roman Thought Still Dominates the Catholic Church

It was Vatican I, in 1869-70, at which only the Latin (and particularly Roman) tradition was taken into consideration, which expressed the doctrine of Roman primacy in terms and concepts which appeared foreign to the Eastern tradition. Vatican II tried to restore a balance but it did not go far enough, for the *rapproachement* between the Catholic and Orthodox Churches requires a new formulation of the doctrine of Roman primacy. This formulation must be grounded in the common tradition of the first thousand years of Christianity, the years preceding the Great Schism. The fact that the Church lived in communion for a thousand years, with the saints and Fathers of the Eastern Churches being venerated (as they are even today) by the Roman Church herself is a powerful argument for unity. This common heritage gives us the framework within which to situate the abstract principles of our ecclesiology. Following the Schism, ecclesiastical development in the Catholic Church took on a Roman-Latin form using Latin, but particularly Roman, formulae and concepts. That these latter cannot today be imposed upon the East is self-evident. This evolution must be explained to the Eastern Churches in terms of those ten preceding centuries of common Church life and not in terms of the later practices of the Western-Latin Church. Any other way of going about this *rapproachement* is bound to fail.

The meeting of Pope Paul and Ecumenical Patriarch Athenagoras in 1964 had such great impact precisely *because* it constituted a return to those contacts which had formerly been the norm between the Church of Rome and the Eastern Churches. The great merit of Paul VI's gesture was that it was not a innovation but rather a restoration of practices which had lain moribund for centuries. Since the Great Schism both the Roman Church and the Eastern Churches had turned in on themselves and on their own values, forgetting the other, and preferring to talk with their own people alone, since for them the other party had, for all practical purposes, ceased to exist.

By reactivating this dialogue, Pope Paul and Patriarch Athenagoras breached the historical gap between the united Church of old and the repentant Church of today. But in order for this dialogue to be efficacious each Church must, for the moment, cease affirming and reaffirming itself in order to discover in the other that which is lacking for its own completeness and perfection. This applies in the realm of theology, liturgy, Scripture, missions, or ecclesiology, etc. Vatican II helped to prepare this dialogue while attempting to avoid a mere repetition of the First Vatican Council.

The Church's Infallibility

The Church is neither more infallible nor more vigilant after the Schism than she was before it. So therefore, all the doctrine and discipline of the ancient Eastern Church during the thousand years of union (during which there was no objection on the part of the Popes or the Ecumenical Councils) have acquired, so to speak, full citizenship in the

Church. Hence, the Catholic Church can never declare itself - by either a Roman or conciliar decree - to be opposed to such and such a doctrine or practice from the East, for it had fully respected them in the first millenium of its own existence, as we have already seen.

In the second session of the Second Vatican Council, we raised the argument *apropos* of the episcopal college and the institution of the patriarchate, both of which - having been a living tradition in the East since the first thousand years of this era - have been recognized and lived also by the patriarchal Church in the West. What we have said applies to all Churches of both the East and West, namely that only a representative Council that brings together Catholics and Orthodox can bring about changes in tradition, whether this be tradition common to both Churches, or proper only to the Christian East.

The Growth of the Roman Primacy

The Primacy is a gift of God to the Church. This will not be denied by anyone. Our Lord did and said nothing lightly, and surely it was not for nothing that He put Peter at the head of the Apostles and bade him confirm his brethren. But Christ never intended to make this "*tu es Petrus*"2 the center and acme of revealed doctrine. *Christ never intended to substitute the head of the apostolic college for the Head of the Church, who can only be the Lord Himself.* It is partly because this has been lost sight of that this primacy, which Christ wanted to be bond of unity and a means of progress, finally became through the fault of men a pretext for division and an obstacle to progress. How did this come about?

In order to understand this evolution, all we need do is observe the fact that nearly all the problems and snags at the Second Vatican Council came about in the name and under the pretext of the primacy of Rome. From the beginning of that Council until its adjournment, all the directing agencies in the Catholic Church have had, as head and core, men "obsessed" with the Roman primacy. They have proven themselves to be opposed to any evolution in the Church, in any and every field - liturgy, and ecclesiology, ecumenism, etc. This group of churchmen, in other respects most worthy men, were adamantly opposed (*a priori and in principle*) to any attempt at evolution within the Church or to any opening up of the Church to the Christian world. They were prompt to use any means possible in order to sabotage the conciliar assembly.

And so it was that the Ecumenical Council which Christianity in all ages has always had the greatest respect for as being the authentic and infallible expression of the Church, came to be considered suspect by the minority, in the name of the primacy and on the pretext of defending it. And when we consider that this minority has had until now the *exclusive* privilege of gorverning the Catholic Church everywhere through the Roman Dicasteries, we can easily appreciate how primacy (in itself and in its application) became an obstacle to any evolution within the Church and to the cause of reconciliation among Christians. There can be no serious progress along these lines as long as the actual government of the Catholic Church has not been wholly and uncopromisingly transferred from the hands of this minority to those of the *pastoral* Episcopate, the only agent truly responsible for the Church of Jesus Christ.

There is yet another argument that can be brought to bear in support of our thesis which is also taken from the day-to-day events at the Council. A minority of the Council Fathers persistently invoked the juridical authority of the Bishop of Rome, in the name of Roman primacy, as prevailing over the mystery of Communion. These Fathers repeated ad nauseam that the Pope is the bond of unity. Granted. But the visible bond of unity should not make us forget the invisible ones. The exterior organization of the Church should not be substituted for its interior life. Those documents brought forth at the Council which underwent the influence of this minority provide us on every page with proof of this kind of substitution. Here is a typical example: "The Eastern Churches, even though different in respect to rite, liturgy, Church discpline and spiritual heritage" nevertheless enjoy true communion among themselves by the fact that "they are all entrusted to the pastoral government of the Roman Pontiff."[3] In pre-Roman Curia times such a statement would have been judged insufficient, ridiculous, suspect, and even dangerous. Where do we see mention of those spiritual and mystical bonds which unite the Churches despite their diversity? Where in these lofty (*sic*) thoughts do we find Jesus Christ, His Divine Life, the sacraments, the same Eucharist, the same sacrifice, the same priesthood?

Furthermore, where is the episcopate established by Jesus Christ to govern the Church (in union with Peter, of course)? It is our understanding of Church history and Tradition that the Church is to be governed by the bishops who are in communion with the Pope, but not exclusively *by* the Pope to the exclusion of the Episcopate. But we will not insist on this point here, for it is not now the main argument.

The Second Council of the Vatican laid the groundwork but we must now call upon the Pope to restore the balance between the Church as a visible society and the Church as a Mystical Body, between its exterior organization and its interior divine life, between the head of the episcopal body and the Head of the Church, between the Pope, servant of the servants of God, and Jesus Christ, the Son of God and God Himself. For it is the sign of an unhealthy obsession to insist upon the diversity of the Churches in the areas of Liturgy, spiritual heritage, etc., and then to make their legitimacy wholly dependent upon the pastoral rule of the Pope. Furthermore, the curialists deny the unity these Churches have among themselves anyway, stating that their *only* bond of union is their common submission to the "pastoral government of the Roman Pontiff."

The Historical Perspective

Catholics must not neglect the historical facts. In the East the rank of patriarchate, which was originally reserved to the five principal sees of Christendom, was extended to other primatial dioceses. The reverse happened in the West. The patriarchate was reduced to a mere honorific title when popes decided to confer it upon certain hierarchs, thereby creating the titular patriarchs of the West. Finally, the West confered this dignity upon these certain Latin bishops whose sees were not such as would normally justify a patriarchate. The result was twofold: the instituting of a *false* patriarchate and the stripping of the original patriarchal office of its essentials.

Today, the Catholic Church, especially the Latin Church, should reassess its idea of the Pariarchal institution.[4] This Church must *cease* to see the extension of this office to the lower Latin clergy as a legitimate and normal development, for this counterfeit sort of patriarchate could become the pretext for leveling all the great sees of the East to an artificial, equalized patriarchal dignity for which there is no basis in history.

Though the five principal Sees of Christian antiquity (Rome, Constantinople, Alexandria, Antioch and Jerusalem) were given the title of patriarchate by the Ecumenical Councils, these sees do not owe their eminent dignity to the titles themselves. On the contrary, *the patriarchal title was simply a sign of recognition of their already existing dignity*. In order to reduce these five sees to the same level as all those others which have received the title over the centuries, it would have to be demonstrated that all these sees had been raised to this dignity for the same reasons, and to an identical degree. Now this has certainly not been the case. For those Western sees claiming to be patriarchates (except for Rome) the question does not even arise, as the title was given them honorifically. As for the Eastern sees made patriarchates at a relatively recent date, they do furnish the necessary conditions for an authentic patriarchate, because they are Mother Churches. Yet even they cannot pretend to be elevated to the same dignity as the older, traditional patriarchates because the newer patriarchates are Mother Churches only on a local or national level, whereas the five older patriarchates were and always will be the Mother Churches of universal Christianity.

Let us consider these Churches now as East and West. History reveals that Rome "created" the Church of the West, while the Churches of the East were either "created" by Constantiople, Alexandria, Antioch or Jerusalem or branched out from them. On the universal plane, then, Rome and the four venerable Eastern patriarchates *together* created the Christian Church in its entirety.

Jerusalem was the cradle of Christianity and the first gathering place for the *apostolic* "Ecumenical" Council. It is the Mother Church of all who believe in Christ. In it are located the sacred places where Jesus was born, lived, preached, died, rose from the dead and ascended into heaven. It remains the first and constant witness to the redemption and offers to the world the Gospel as it was lived, written on its very soil, for it is an irrefutable illustration of the written Gospels. City of the bloody Sacrifice and the first unbloody Liturgy, Jerusalem is forever present wherever a Christian altar is raised and the Eucharist is celebrated. Mother of all the Christian Churches, Jerusalem is also sacred to every Muslim and Jew.

Antioch, also called "the City of God", was the first See of Peter, the first missionary Church to preach the Good News abroad, and the first to found Churches which were in turn to become missionary Churches. Antioch was, in earlier times, the most famous capital in all the East. Its theology and liturgy were to profoundly influence the faith and piety of all Christianity.

And Alexandria, named after Alexander the Great - how much the universal Church owes to its famous theological school and to its holy Fathers! And as for monasticism, are not the most evolved and varied monastic rules of the West as well as the East mere adaptations of the monasticism formed and lived in Egypt by Pachomius, Anthony the Great and their disciples?

Constantinople was made the extension of Rome, its other self, and even named "the new Rome". So many Churches owe it their existence and how many more would have died out without Constantinople? Let us recall the seven great Ecumenical Councils, the main pillars of our faith. Were they not held at Constantinople or within its territorial influence (Nicaea, Ephesus, Chalcedon)? Constantinople did not furnish merely the geographical location for these councils but, along with the other traditional patriarchal sees of the East, it gave to these conciliar assemblies the immense majority of their Fathers and theologians who brilliantly stated and defined the Christian faith for all ages.

Certainly Constantinople, Alexandria, Antioch and Jerusalem, along with Rome, are the Source-Churches of all the others. Now this is not merely indulging in archaeologizing or in self-aggrandizement, for what would have become of the Christian East without Constantinople? Along with Rome, the four Eastern sees still remain the principal protectors of the Christian faith. Orthodoxy still considers these major sees as much, and - with the Ecumenical Patriarch at their head - they are presented at Pan-Orthodox conferences as being the summit of the episcopacy.[5]

To want to amalgamate the four patriarchs of Orthodoxy with all the other patriarchs in some sort of artificial patriarchal equality would be an act of injustice and aggression as well as of stupidity, and certainly foreign to the attitudes of the late Pope John XXIII. It would be tantamount to decapitating the Eastern Churches in order to submit them to the undemocratic, authoritarian control of the Roman Curia. In that case it would be absurd to have dialog with Orthodoxy, for a common ground would simply not exist. Were this done, we frankly do not see how a common ground could ever be regained.

In conclusion, all men of good will cannot but call upon the Roman Catholic Church to *prove* the veracity of those eloquent statements made by many of its leaders during the last few hundred years. What especially comes to mind is a quotation from a pronouncemnet of Pope Benedict XV who lived during the First World War, "The Church of Jesus Christ is neither Latin nor Greek nor Slav, but Catholic; accordingly it makes no distinction between its children, for Greeks, Latins, Slavs and members of all other nations are equal in the eyes of the [Roman] Apostolic See."

Notes

1. In this connection, I can only lament the document of the Second Vatican Council entitled: *Orientalium Ecclesiarum* which did all the Eastern Churches many injustices. Its very first words seem to indicate that we Eastern Catholics are second class citizens in the Church Universal, for it reads: "The *Catholic* Church holds in esteem the institutions, liturgical rites, ecclesiastical traditions and the norms of ... the *Eastern* Churches ..." This implies that the *Catholic* Church is the *Latin* Church alone!

2. "You are Peter, and on this rock I will build my Church." (Matthew 16, 18)

3. *Orientalium Ecclesiarum*, 3.

4. In December 1969, Pope Paul VI appointed Archbishop Albino Luciani the new Latin Patriarch of Venice, a post that had been vacant since the death of Giovanni Cardinal Urbani three months earlier. Had Pope Paul abolished this Latin Patriarchate or, at least, used a term as "minor Patriarchate", the Christian Orient would have rejoiced. Such an action would give the Catholic world the impetus and new opportunity to reevaluate the institution of the patriarchate. [R.B.]

5. The late Patriarch Alexis I of Moscow, who was the spiritual leader of by far the most numerous Orthodox Church, did not hesitate to prostrate himself before the late Patriarch Christopher of Alexandria when they met a few years ago. Nor would he, even though head of the strongest and largest of the newer patriarchal Churches, have hesitated to do the same were he to have met the Patriarch of Constantinople, Alexandria, Antioch or Jerusalem.

Eight - The Second Vatican Council and Unity

What concerned us most, as Eastern Christians, at the Second Vatican Council was the work being accomplished toward the reunion of Eastern and Western Christianity. Every believer in Christ surely was, and is, concerned with unity, but the question touches us Eastern Catholics far more deeply than either Western Catholics or Eastern Orthodox. Why is this so?

Both these Churches, Eastern and Western, enjoy a certain wholeness as completely constituted entities, with their own life, their Apostolic origins and their solidly established traditions. From the age of the great Ecumenical Councils, they have agreed with each other, sometimes disagreed, as often as not ignored each other, each living in her own world like twin sisters having her own home, her own self-sufficiency, and her independence.

These sister-churches would undoubtedly be greatly enriched by reuniting, thereby realizing the will of Christ for unity. Yet even while remaining apart each has her own home, her own liturgies, her own theology, her own patristic teaching, laws and traditions.

But in our case as Eastern Catholics, we were born in Orthodoxy and raised in Catholicism. We love our Mother, and remain attached to our Father. We are like children of separated parents. We cannot live in Orthodoxy without missing our Father deeply nor can we rest and abide in Catholicism without constantly searching for our absent Mother. We will be to find both of them only in a reunited home, the reunited Church. Until such time no Eastern Catholic Community can expect to find its final place in what is called Uniatism. Uniatism is, after all, merely a temporary state and no matter how comfortable these communities may think they are in it, they must constantly bear in mind Uniatism's transitory nature. To forget the latter would be to betray their very mission.

In a pre-Vatican II letter issued by our late Patriarch Maximos IV, we read: "A union of the Churches undoubtedly represents a grave and vital problem for a good number of bishops. However, they are only looking at this issue from a theoretical point of view. *We are the ones who feel the division as a bleeding wound, a constant and deep sorrow*. The problem of union is our greatest concern, our primary preoccupation, our deepest and most heartfelt desire. We work and strain towards this goal with all our strength, desiring and willing to be the redemptive victim if only our hopes be realized. In fact, this is our very mission, our *raison d'etre*, which Providence has enjoined upon Eastern Catholics, both individually and collectively..."

At the Second Vatican Council we laid aside everything that could be called our exclusive problem in order to channel all our energies into the cause of union. We have concentrated all our attention on the Churches of the East. We have endeavored to make them better known and loved, to make their customs and traditions more widely esteemed because we feel that this esteem is absolutely necessary for a truly serious and effectual dialogue with Orthodoxy.

But even if the Second Vatican Council was not called specifically to solve the problem of East-West Union it was, nevertheless, bound to prepare the way. This is, in fact, what it did during all four sessions. Now, I would like to explain how the Council contributed to a rapprochement of Christians. Kindly bear with me while I emphasize the rapprochement between Catholics and Orthodox, since the East is, after all, almost exclusively Orthodox.

The very announcement by Pope John of a worldwide Council of Bishops evoked a favorable response from Orthodox Church leaders. (Eastern Christianity has always had a predilection for synodal meetings because the *magisterium* in such gatherings is exercised through the collegial power of the bishops meeting in council.[1]) The Orthodox Churches had seen the Catholic Church depart ever farther from the collegial tradition during the past few hundred years, especially since the First Vatican Council. The Roman doctrine of the primacy and infallibility of the Bishop of Rome took on monumental proportions and its development in the life of the Church was considerably detrimental to the individual and collective power of the bishops. The fact of a conciliar meeting produced a feeling of relief for both Orthodox and Catholics since such a council constitutes a recognition of the very fact of episcopal collegiality. Undoubtedly certain Orthodox cannot conceive of a council being genuinely Ecumenical when only Catholic bishops (being almost all Latins) are present, anymore than they could conceive of a Council being Ecumenical without the presence of the Bishop of Rome.

Out of nearly twenty-five hundred Council Fathers there were only 130 non-Latin bishops and the bishops representing some 250 million Orthodox Christians were conspicuously absent. Their absence was a source of great discomfort to us. Yet in spite of our small numbers, while we were at the Council we tried to insist upon our common bonds with our Orthodox brethren. We believe we truly succeeded in large measure thanks to the many courageous stands taken by our truly Oriental bishops[2] and thanks also to our great liturgical riches. The Oriental Catholic liturgies were able to reveal so much of the majestic beauty inherent in the Eastern Churches with such effect that this Council has been called "the Epiphany of the East."

And so, the very fact of this Council is an application of the principal of collegial episcopal power and is, by the same token, an opening up to ecumenism.

The majority of the Council Fathers came to Rome, in the first place, with the firm intention of reaching a common definition of episcopal power and of making the Catholic Church more universal and more conciliar. To some extent they succeeded brilliantly. Witness just these few words from a speech of the late Archbishop of Montreal, Paul Emile Cardinal Leger: "The Council will not end. The Church has become conciliar once again. The bishops will be meeting more often - both in Rome and in their own regional episcopal synods."

Now this point precisely is very important for union. As they insist upon the collegial power of the Apostles, the Orthodox Churches evolve towards an ever greater autonomy; whereas the Catholic Church over the last few centuries, and above all since the First Vatican Council, has been evolving in the opposite direction, towards centralization. Catholics and Orthodox will be able to reunite only by finding a balance in mutual harmony. Vatican II, by clearly setting forth the powers of the bishops, has thus begun to promote decentralization and prepare the way for unity.

This is why the bishops insisted on making the chapter on the Church and the Episcopacy the masterpiece of all the Conciliar documents. Indeed, it was our late Patriarch Maximos IV who, in one of his speeches since become famous, seeing that too much time was being spent on other less significant chapters, asked that the Fathers "proceed with no further delay" to the chapter "On the Church," to clarify and define the respective places of the Episcopacy, the clergy, and the faithful in the Church. For, as he explained, "Since 1870 (the date of the conclusion of the First Vatican Council) the Church has resembled a sort of dwarf with an enormous head, and a tiny body." He insisted upon giving more attention to "developing the body in proportion to the head."

It was therefore necessary to define the power of the Episcopacy. This meant studying the powers of the bishop in his own diocese, examining the powers of the bishops meeting in Synods or in national and regional councils and looking into the powers of the bishops meeting in Ecumenical Council.

Why was it considered necessary to restore the episcopal powers in the Catholic Church? There are several reasons; some dogmatic, others practical. One aim was to encourage union with the separated Churches, who had remained faithful to the principle of local episcopal power.

It was necessary, in the first place, to restore episcopal power because such was the will of Christ who founded the Apostolic College. For the Pope is not, in fact, the only bishop in the Church; he is its *first* bishop. Christ gave the "presidency" of the Apostolic College to Peter only *after* having entrusted all the Apostles with a clear-cut, well-defined mission. The leader of the Apostles was designated, then, to be head of a College which had already been constituted, a College already enjoying authentic and inalienable powers. Saint Peter was a member of this College when he received the mission of strengthening his brethren. It is easy to conclude, therefore, that episcopal power does not emanate from the Bishop of Rome but is a power constituted by divine law and received directly from Christ. The Council Fathers then, wished to re-establish this power in fact, first of all because it was the will of Jesus Himself.

Secondly, it was necessary to restore the episcopal powers because in so doing adequate meaning is thereby given to the primacy of the Bishop of Rome. Elementary logic tells us that in order for one bishop to be prime bishop, there must exist other bishops. So, the very primacy of the Pope presupposes the existence of an episcopal college with its own statutory rights. If this were not so, of whom would he be "the first"? If he is the first bishop in Christendom, this means that there are also other bishops. And if the latter can only make suggestions and execute orders, then the primary becomes meaningless.

The powers of the bishops had to be restored, in the third place, in order to protect the successors of the Apostles (i.e. the bishops) against abusive encroachments. It is this college of bishops (and not the Roman Congregations, whose members seem to live in a world divorced from the rest of humanity), yes, the bishops themselves who must assume the responsibilities in the Church.[3]

Returning to our list we see that the fourth reason for restoring these powers, as was briefly mentioned above, is that no dialogue with Orthodoxy is possible until episcopal rights are clearly enumerated. Whether or not it be true, we have heard ecumenical experts say that the primacy of Rome is not irreconcilable with collegial episcopal power. Proceeding on this premise we find that the Catholic Church will being going contrary to public opinion and to the principals of ecumenism if she continues to withhold even one of the bishops' rightful prerogatives.

We have seen then, that the Second Vatican Council has contributed to the rapprochement of the Catholic and Orthodox Churches because the very fact of the Council is already an implicit affirmation of the collegial episcopal power and because by defining this power more explicitly, the council Fathers have made the Catholic Church more universal and more conciliar and, therefore, more open to union.

But there is yet another important reason. Owing, on the one hand, to Catholic centralization, which considerably reduces the role of the Episcopacy, clergy and faithful in the Church; and owing, on the other hand, to Orthodox decentralization, which often makes the heads of the different communities absolute masters in their own churches, Christian unity until now was conceived of as an official act alone, the affair of the hierarchy and a matter for a summit conference of the heads of the differing Christian groups. It thus seemed that unity depended wholly upon their own good-will or upon their self interests (which often would even be in opposition!). The clergy and faithful could hope and pray for this union or urge it only from the sidelines, as if it were really not their business or their real concern. Seen in this light, union became a matter of mere human compromise; an "understanding" to be reached by the leaders of the Churches and to be imposed on the clergy and faithful. Such a union, being only the fruit of diplomacy or human maneuvering, is bound to fail because it does not follow the will of the Master.

When the Churches have reintegrated all the members of the Mystical Body into the totality of their life; when the least significant member of the faithful can *act*, not just pray, in the cause of unity - in collaboration with his pastor, bishop and patriarch, not simply as a subordinate who must obey, but as a living member in the Body of Christ sharing with all the members (as well as with the head) the same life and same responsibility in proportion to his role - then and only then will union become a supernatural reality binding together the whole Body and benefitting from all the divine graces and energies which are communicated through the Savior to all members of His Mystical Body.

How often have we heard: "If only Christian unity were left to the people, it would have been realized years ago."? I would like to add a few important words to that saying: "If Christian unity were up to the people and to their spiritual leaders it would have been realized long ago." Vatican II began the program to reintegrate all the clergy and all the people into the entire day-to-day life of the church, thereby preparing the road for unity. The Second Vatican Council's wish was to eliminate the dichotomy between priests and people, truly making one body of both groups, for this is what is meant by the phrase "the People of God."

In the Council's final document on the powers of the bishops, the principle of decentralization was vigorously upheld, and was later applied to the chapter on the (Roman) liturgy, and from then on commanded the discussion of the other schemas on the agenda.[4] The Council Fathers asserted that Christian unity does not mean uniformity, that union does not mean the absorption of one Church by another. They reaffirmed that each Church must preserve her own authentic personality, customs and traditions in the reunited Church. The Fathers declared, furthermore, that the Eastern Churches can be reunited with the Western Church without being swallowed up by it. On the contrary, this union would enrich the Catholic Church as much as the Orthodox Churches.

At the Council I said that the problem of Christian unity is not the same for the Orthodox as for the Protestants. This is true because the relationship between the Latin Church and the Orthodox Churches is essentially different from the one between the Roman-Latin Church and the Protestant groups. In the final analysis one will find that the Protestants broke off from their Mother, the Latin Church; they were born in her, and were part and parcel of her.

As for the Eastern Churches, even if they did not always recognize the primacy of the bishop of Rome in the manner he would have wished, everyone should face the fact that the Eastern Churches were never a part of the Latin Church. Taken as a whole, the Eastern Churches are *sister Churches* of the Latin Church. Their existence does not emanate from the Latin Church any more than do their subsistence or developing of dogma and discipline. The Eastern Churches, and therefore the Orthodox Church, are historically *source* Churches just as much as the Latin Church is a source Church for the West. Founded by the Apostles and their immediate disciples, they were born without the concourse of the West, since their discipline and liturgies are quite distinct from those of the West. Their very doctrine, while essentially the same as that of the Latin Church, has been assimilated and lived out in a different manner: to witness, those Fathers the Greek Church whose works lie side by side with those of the Latin Fathers on everyone's bookshelves but which are never confused with the Latins' theology.

The Eastern and Western Churches exhibit different spirits and different but authentic Christian inspirations, each tracing itself back to the living source which is Christ, but traveling thence over different terrain, through civilizations and national temperaments of distinctly different nature, and so possessing different and often irreducible characteristics.

We cannot forget this unique situation without running the risk of seeing the separation as a mere tantrum on the part of the East. No, this truth must be fully understood by all, in order to envisage correctly the if's, and's and how's of reunion.

Let us not deceive ourselves. It is not men who make Councils, nor is it their passions, their maneuvering, their intelligence or their knowledge which lead the Church. It is the Holy Spirit, whose action has been so evident. God has blessed the Second Vatican Council through the good-will and sincerity of the Council Fathers - all of them; those who looked to the future being distrustful of the past, those who looked to the past being distrustful of the future, and those who had already achieved a happy balance of the two.

The Holy Spirit was at work in all; through the Council Fathers themselves and through all who prayed and labored for the Council and for the works of unity and peace. From now on, being more fully integrated into the Mystical Body of Christ, all will be able to work together not only for their own salvation but for the salvation of the entire world.

Notes

1. This is clearly evident in the Joint Declaration of Paul VI and Athenagoras I concerning the schism between the Greek and Latin Churches. Each reference in the statement ascribes their joint action to "Pope Paul VI and Patriarch Athenagoras I with his Synod". [F.S.]

2. If anyone would doubt the authenticity of the statement that "Greek Catholics are *Orthodox who happen to be united to Rome*", we can refer him to Orthodox Patriarch Athenagoras' words addressed to the late Melkite Greek Catholic Patriarch Maximos IV: "You are our voice at the Council; the voice of our common hopes, and the voice of the East."

3.   To digress for a moment, I would like to impress upon the reader that we Eastern Catholics still have not forgotten the "new" Code of Eastern Canon Law promulgated under Pope Pius XII. One passage (out of many strange or stranger) in this "code" grants the nuncio or Apostolic Delegate (even when he is *not* a bishop) precedence over the bishops and patriarchs, even when the latter are in their own dioceses! As one can easily gather, we Easterners have found it impossible to admit this reversal of the order established by Jesus Christ Himself! Surely this action itself was sufficient to make the union of Eastern and Western Christianity unthinkable!

4. These were: "On Christian Unity", and "On the Church".

Part IV - Uniatism

Nine - Uniatism and Ecumenism

Some of the Fathers at Vatican Council II, listening to the wise and lucid speeches of the late Melkite Greek Catholic Patriarch Maximos IV and his bishops, could well have been tempted to remark, as did one non-Catholic observer: "Your Patriarch and your bishops speak as men having authority."[1]

At a Council, every validly ordained bishop and successor of the Apostles has the undeniable right to speak with authority and it is with this same common, traditional authority received from Jesus Christ, that our bishops have spoken and acted at the Second Vatican Council. We have tried not to gain publicity or to stand out for our own individual benefit as some may suppose. We sincerely believe that a worldwide Council is a very serious and all too rare event which places a grave obligation on the Church and all who participate. Consequently, it should not be used for personal gain.

All we intended to do is to perform a duty of conscience made all the more pressing by the fact that we are Uniates. As will soon be demonstrated, it is not for the purpose of glorifying it that we made Uniatism assume a particular responsibility at the Council.

A Serious Obligation to Speak

We had an obligation to speak often and boldly at the Second Vatican Council because all sides of the issues discussed had to be allotted equal time or a balance of viewpoints would not be achieved. A further obligation belonged to our bishops because we, as Uniates, realize that Uniatism is not a definitive formula for unity nor does it represent a third Christian unit to be added to both traditional kinds of Christianity, the Latin and the Orthodox, not to speak of Protestantism. Uniatism is a mere experiment in unity. Its one and only concern should be to hasten the hour of reconciliation and of integration into Orthodoxy within the reunited Church.

Let us put it another way: *Uniatism is not a final situation but merely a temporary stage* which, related to the problem of Christian unity, can contribute to its solution only by going beyond itself to confront the whole of divided Christianity.

I would like to explain further: the unity to which Eastern Christians are aspiring is that will reconcile the Catholic Church of the West, which is nearly totally Latin, with the Churches of the East, 95% of which are Orthodox. Being Uniates we are neither Latin nor Orthodox. If we claim ours to be an ecumenical mission, it is in all modesty that we will have to fulfill it, since it is our *primary* task. Since we are not a real "party" in the conflict that opposes Latin Christianity and Orthodoxy but simply *witnesses* to a several centuries old unsuccessful experiment, we are not directly involved. The problem of Christian unity is still before the Churches, awaiting a new and lasting solution. Though an experiment be unsuccessful it can, nevertheless, provide some enrichment and some valuable lessons. Our Uniate experiment can open up for others chances for success which Uniatism itself did not offer. Nobody then should have been astonished to see the eagerness of our Eastern Christian Bishops in grasping such a rare and almost unique opportunity which the Second Vatican Council constituted. It was our intention to reformulate the problem of unity in the light of our own Uniate experiment and to help the Council Fathers clearly understand the obstacles that have so often confronted the Uniates. For many years prior to the Council we repeatedly wrote and lectured hoping to make it clear that the methods being followed to put an end to the fragmentation of Christianity were totally inadequate. Sometimes we became discouraged because the bureaucracy was so thoroughly engaged in a one-way Catholicism. We welcomed the conciliar assembly of Vatican II because we hoped that it would afford us a genuine opportunity to present our case to the many open-minded bishops.

The serious problem of Christian unity was, and still is, a problem which is beyond our power as Uniates to resolve. We have simply wanted to make available to the assembled Catholic Episcopate the rather negative results of an experiment of union we ourselves have lived for a long time, together with our suggestions and proposals for more effective action. Even though the Latin Episcopate was the majority, they had the obligation to listen to us because Christian unity is, in the first place, their concern. It is their business, an unfinished business between them and Orthodoxy, a business produced by a schism that has separated the Eastern Churches and the Church of Rome. Moreover, a large number of Conciliar Fathers naturally depended on the Uniates to prepare the way for unity and some of them have even though that since the creation of Uniatism the problem had already been solved. Proof of this is to be found in this: for centuries everyone left the application of this solution to the Uniates. Accordingly, we Uniates owed the bishops, and also the whole Catholic Church, an unbiased and clear explanation of the *real* nature and the *transitory* state of Uniatism, a report on Uniatism and the Uniate Churches' progress to date, and an exposition of the present state of relations between an *Eastern* Orthodoxy and a *Latin* Catholicism. In trying to define our role as unifiers, we must briefly recall the birth and history of Uniatism.

The History of Uniatism

Uniates are Eastern Christians who, in the relatively recent past (due to the influence of the Crusaders and Latin missionaries, and to being in contact with Catholic nations), have found conditions favorable for their abandoning of Orthodoxy and adhering to the Roman Catholic Church. The Holy See of Rome has given them a new hierarchy independent of the Orthodox one and has reorganized them into communities distinct from the Christendom they had heretofore known. They were also given both moral and material assistance from the West. The new secular and religious culture which has accompanied the budding and blossoming of their Uniatism and which has succeeded in distinguishing them from their Orthodox brethren, was greatly influenced by Latin missionaries. In spite of an often heroic dedication, these Roman missionaries to the East were unable to give anything else than that which they themselves already had and were.

Although they retained their Eastern liturgy and were endowed with the same traditional patriarchal and other titles as the Orthodox hierarchy, the Uniates received a human, theological and ascetical formation inspired by the Occidental and Latin traditions. Things could hardly have been different, for Catholicism had never assimilated the spirit of authentic Eastern Christendom and was not attuned to it as a consequence. *The Uniates joined Rome at a time when the matter of unity was not being considered in an ecumenical perspective* as had been done at the council of Florence and as it would be later on. The Latin missionaries took an interest in their immediate "ex-Orthodox" disciples without actually coming to grips with those things that constitute the essence of Orthodoxy. Being the benefactors of the Uniates in the social and cultural areas the missionaries had become, to a certain extent, their fathers in the faith; they had *given* them their own Latin Catholicism ready made, prefabricated, and only superficially adapted to them, i.e. adapted in externals alone. This is how our liturgies and hierarchical structures have been preserved while in reality being subordinated to the Roman dicasteries.

Our deeper religious culture came to us, the Uniates, by means of Latin textbooks, the only texts possessed by our Western Catholic teachers. A long time had to elapse before it became possible to blend anything Eastern into our studies. Ignorant about our own good things, the missionaries were eager to give us the best of their own. This is how the prosperous and generous Latins envisioned union. They thought that after having given us so much of what they are, we would turn out to be the leaven in the mass of our Eastern brethren. However, this did not happen. It cannot be denied that the contribution of the Latin Catholics has been valuable as far as culture and social betterment are concerned. I emphasize the fact that Uniate communities benefitted by a remarkable spiritual renewal, thanks to Latin religious schools and seminaries and to the intensive apostolic activity of the missionaries. Religious practice (Latin oriented, of course) has increased and works of charity have been expanded.

Uniatism has developed within the very narrow limits of individuals and groupings rather than on the ecumenical level of the Churches. This has isolated us [Uniates] and has thwarted our efforts towards union. Cut off by his social Christian environment, the Uniate has found himself facing his fellow countrymen of the same rite from within an embarrassing minority party. We should not loose sight of the fact that in certain countries with an Orthodox majority, *belonging to the local Church coincides with participating in the nationality of the country* and that in those countries, the Uniate (who has left the traditional Church of his rite) has been unfairly classified as someone foreign. This treatment has perhaps been justified to some degree because many of the Uniates themselves have sometimes substituted a Western and Latin culture for their own local and regional religious traditions and, occasionally even modified the norms to which their Eastern Christianity had been attuned. The exposure of the Uniates to the vexations and discriminations aimed at their various sensitivities has hindered the normal development of their social and public life.

Not only has Uniatism cut off these Eastern Christians from their Churches of origin, but Uniatism has made each member appear as a provocation to Orthodoxy and as a challenge to be faced.

Every time an Eastern Uniate Church is created, a new hierarchy is, in fact, set up alongside of, and in real competition with, the locally established Orthodox hierarchy. The new Uniate hierarchy is generally adorned with the identical prerogatives borne by their Orthodox counterparts.[2]

Uniatism Needs "Re-Orthodoxization"

In facing such a painful situation, Uniatism needed to confront all the accusations with a traditional Eastern physiognomy. Recognizing this, some of the staunchest defenders of its Eastern traditions have been none other than the Roman Pontiffs themselves! Papal documents such as *Orientalium Dignitas* of Pope Leo XIII, show the great esteem in which their authors held the Eastern Churches. These documents also show the official papal opposition to the Latinization of Eastern Catholics. But the results of these few papal efforts have not been sufficient. Why? Because the problem did not consist so much in preventing Latinization as in activating a de-Latinization program, or better, in returning the Orthodox ways of thought and religious attitudes to the Easterners who had entered Catholicity through the Latin gate. The missionaries who had been the originators of the Uniatism we have described, could not themselves be the agents of re-Orthodoxization.[3] Moreover, the instructions issued by the popes and their repeated warnings could not reach the heart of the matter, nor could they rebuild Uniatism on a better foundation. These papal warnings were aimed mostly at preventing all attacks on the integrity of the Eastern rites and to prohibit Orthodox from entering the Catholic Church via the Latin rite, as was a practice during certain historical periods. As for the thorough Latinizing of Eastern Christian thought in schools and seminaries, little was done to remedy this until recent years, for the missionaries in charge of those establishments were generally more virtuous and zealous than competent in Eastern Christian thought. More important than that, the cause of the evil - I apologize for having to use that term - the cause of the evil not having been eliminated, the efforts put forth by those well-intentioned popes to safeguard the liturgical rites and to help the Uniates retain their original Eastern customs have achieved only mediocre results.

Not long ago, I was present in a Uniate Catholic parish church where an Eastern Eucharistic Liturgy was being celebrated. We heard the celebrant say *his* "Mass" as low as could be, while a young lady was singing pious French hymns from the choir loft even though the music bore no relation whatever to the Liturgy. In the framework of traditional Eastern Christianity such a Liturgy, whether objectively valid or invalid, has the same effect as heresy. Despite the threat of the severest of papal censures, the Latin missionaries continued the practice of Latinizing the Orthodox ways of the people.

Nevertheless, the new Eastern Catholic Code of Canon Law,[4] after centuries of the popes' own struggles against Latinization, leads us back to the very same starting point. Canon 11, paragraph 1, says the following: "The non-Catholic baptized person of the Eastern rite, on reception into the Catholic Church, *may embrace the rite of his choice*[5] [including the Latin rite]; it is preferable however, that they retain their own rite." If the most severe threats have not produced the desired results these amiably expressed wishes can be expected to produce even fewer results.[6]

This change of attitude should not astonish us. One cannot expect the road to be easy after a bad start. The popes are not miracle workers; they cannot change the laws of nature. Born and developed under the Latin sun, Uniatism cannot escape its native climate if it is to survive. All treatments that have been applied to it are only palliatives whose effects are but temporary and superficial. As I have said again and again: Uniatism must be freed from all tutelage and be restored in an ecumenical climate. It has to be de-Latinized and it must recover its Orthodox mode of living. Why? Because the only opportunity for Uniatism to fulfill its mission as unifier lies in its capacity to familiarize the Western Catholic Church, for many years isolated from any contact with real Eastern Christianity, with Orthodox ecclesiastical institutions - institutions which Uniates have had to "live" in the very bosom of a Western Catholicity. Instead of being retained by the Uniates in their pure forms, these venerable institutions have been adapted to Latin concepts. Such a procedure distorted them and still renders them incapable of creating a common atmosphere where Latin Christianity and Orthodoxy can rediscover each other.

Uniatism Is Out of Date

Uniatism has passed out of date. It is unable to solve the problem of unity. And, contrary to what some may think, unity has not been achieved merely because these Eastern Uniate communities exist within Catholicism. Why?

The Catholic Church, now in the midst of an evolution of monumental proportions and significance, is still searching for a just formula that will lead to an ecumenical Christian unity. Fortunately, it is no longer satisfied with a Uniatism that pries loose individuals or groups from the body of Orthodoxy in order to set them up in distinct Churches. This amounts to *separating* for the purpose of *uniting*. Such an outdated method no longer responds to the exigencies of real ecumenism. This is so for various reasons, among them:

a.) it realizes union only in *a very restricted way* because it leads Eastern Christian minorities into the Catholic Church. Though I do not wish to offend any Uniates, I am compelled to admit that we Uniates will always be of relatively little importance when compared to the whole of Orthodoxy;

b.) it achieves union only in a *superficial way* because Uniatism is a union of individuals, not a union of Churches with different ecclesial and patristic traditions into a universal Catholicism;

c.) it achieves union *imperfectly* because Uniatism thrives only at the expense of collective unity. Instead of uniting, it creates within Orthodox Christianity the same type of separations that occurred when the Protestants withdrew from their Mother Church of the West, but in a different direction. The mending of the Uniate-Orthodox schisms would be of infinitely greater ecumenical value than to encourage a few individuals to separate from Orthodox Christianity.

Although acknowledging the right of individuals to adopt the formula of faith dictated by their consciences, the Catholic Church seems to have matured, for it no longer wishes to base its ecumenical activity on what is called "individual conversions".

It would be better to negotiate one day the reunion among Churches at a new - and just - Council of Florence than to continue to set up Uniate communities in apposition to the legitimate Orthodox Churches whose creation the latter consider to be hostile acts and whose maintenance is seen as a perpetual act of defiance. With Pope John XXIII, the Second Vatican Council, Patriarch Athenagoras and his confreres, one can soon expect to see a more favorable climate than the one in which the Council of Florence had been held.

The Secretariat for Christian Unity, created in Rome by Pope John and made permanent by Pope Paul VI, has the mission to prepare this climate so as to engage the Catholic Church in a more effective dialogue with Orthodoxy.

The Uniates have a very important role to play as far as unity is concerned. The Arabic proverb says: "Better ask questions of an experienced man than of a smart man." Now then, nobody has felt more acutely than ourselves this unity problem; nobody has experienced more than we its difficulties and known its ambiguities. Nobody has been burdened by the yoke of the Uniate experiment of unity as much as our communities, compelled as they have been to live on the fringe of a powerfully Latin Catholicism and outlawed from an Orthodox society in the eyes of whose members the Uniates are considered "schismatics".

Our role then, is that of a *witness* to a lived experiment of union or that of an experienced *guide* who, having walked the roads of unity, knows the terrain and now endeavors to keep the Church abreast of what is around the next bend lest she stumble. This role is that of a *servant*; therefore, we cannot expect to be one of the two major partners in the negotiations. But we can and do wish to render great assistance (e.g. as we did at the Second Vatican Council) for we, as humble servants, have put at their disposal our experience and we hope that they will consult us frequently in the days that are ahead, for we are quite willing to offer ourselves as a redeeming holocaust for Christian unity.

Uniatism Will Disappear

We do not think that Uniatism will vanish immediately, since Uniatism does not yet seem to be on its way out. But if it is desirable that Uniatism collaborate more efficiently in the task of Christian unity than it has done in the past, the means must be provided to exercise positive action in favor of this unity; this would be done by achieving unity within itself, in greater harmony between Catholicism to which we have acceded and Orthodoxy to which we Uniates belong.

Until now we have been able to serve unity mostly by pointing out the obstacles to be avoided. Unceasingly we have repeated: "this we should not do," "we should react differently," "we should not mistake the Latin Church for the whole Catholic Church," "we should not Latinize," etc. We must now begin to do something more positive such as throwing out all our Latinisms and our Latin patterns of thinking, whether this is approved of or not! We must return *totally* to our Orthodox heritage in our patterns of thinking and in almost every other way or we will be hindering instead of helping the cause of Unity!

Uniatism and Traditional Eastern Institutions

As things now stand, what should be the Uniate attitude toward the traditional Eastern institutions, particularly what should their feelings be toward the patriarchate? They must reevaluate all these things and adopt the position that will serve the cause of unity. In fact:

a) nothing can more reassure the Orthodox regarding the respect of their institutions than seeing these institutions honored and fully alive in Uniatism;

b) even if the Uniate Churches do not involve Orthodoxy, they do involve the Orthodox *institutions* that the Uniates have decided to retain, particularly the institution of the patriarchate whose traditional titles they bear. Erected as patriarchates, the Uniate Churches have to be treated accordingly. Remember: the institution itself is being abused when its titles are;

c) the popes addressed themselves to Uniates as well as to Orthodox Christians[7] when promising to protect the rights and prerogatives of the Eastern Churches. The Uniates have, therefore, the right and the duty to see to it that these promises are kept!

Looking Ahead

After the great day of reunion, the Orthodox Churches will have to give at least as much as they will receive. It is only natural that they be given all the necessary authority and power to protect their own venerable patrimony and the means by which they may transmit it integrally to their own people, including the individual Uniates who will have recently returned to Orthodoxy. The problems between the Latin West and the Orthodox East will be less complicated when we pass the Uniate stage and go on to the stage of mutual acceptance, when the Catholic Church will consider Orthodoxy as a sister instead of a stranger to be converted.

When the Latins in mission countries create a Christian Catholic community they shape it to their own image and give it everything, including new cultural values as well as new religious and moral values. Regretfully, the same procedure has been used by Latin missionaries in Eastern Christian countries which, in effect, treats the Eastern Christians exactly like pagans! As my esteemed brother, Archbishop Joseph Raya, then of Haifa, Nazareth and all Galilee said: "In the Eastern lands, *within* the Catholic Church, alas, segregation is practiced. One group [the Latins] ranks first, and the others live 'from the scraps that fall from their masters' table.'[8]

"How beautiful it would be if the Western missionary Church in its presence in the East would identify with its Eastern sister (are they or are they not sisters?) to help it rediscover its Eastern soul and its true spirit. This would aid the Church to accomplish its mission as messengers of Christ in the midst of all religious, and in the midst of the suspicion which politically splits the Near East."[9]

The preponderant influence of the Latin mind in today's Catholic Church has made of Uniatism a sort of compromise; something which is neither authentically Latin, nor authentically Greek, Coptic, Syrian, Armenian, or Slavic. The reunion, as desired by the more ecumenically oriented Catholic Church, still does not seem to admit of compromise. The Orthodox Churches wish to maintain their patrimony just as they have received it. I sincerely hope that the Latin mind can soon practice the slogan it preaches *a propos* the Eastern Churches, keeping in mind that it is from St. Augustine, one of the West's greatest theologians: "Unity in essential matters, freedom in non-essential matters, but loving charity in everything."

A Pan-Uniate Hierarchy?

Certain Eastern Catholic Churches, whose concern is less with ecumenism and Christian unity than with preserving their own local Uniatism, are now trying to achieve inter-uniatism by attempting to intermingle and amalgamate into one the Uniate hierarchies of the various Eastern Churches united with Rome.[10] Ecumenists and unity-minded hierarchs and people believe that unifying the Uniate Catholic hierarchies means the sanctioning of the anti-ecumenical character of Uniatism. We think that the following will offer a few answers as to why these pan-uniates should abandon their present policies.

First of all, as we have already seen, Uniatism has not actually solved the problem of Christian unity. The matter is only now being brought to the fore by Orthodox and Catholics.

Secondly, Uniatism in itself cannot be a happy or even a possible formula for East-West unity. Bearing in many places the imprint of Latinism, challenging Orthodox Churches by erecting new hierarchies in the face of their traditional ones and by recruiting followers from among the Orthodox faithful; due to all this Uniatism presents itself as being hostile to Orthodoxy and, therefore, is not qualified to be an agent of unity!

Finally, Uniatism needs to be reformed in a way that liberates it from the hostility of the Orthodox and enables it to serve the cause of unity. It has to be delatinized and brought back to its traditional Eastern sources. Within itself, it has to reevaluate the patriarchal and other institutions of Orthodoxy which it has often devaluated by trying to adapt them to Latinism. Uniatism must be reformed to familiarize the Catholic Church with *genuine* Eastern Christian thought and tradition. Uniatism's reform should not be undertaken in order to oppose Eastern Orthodoxy with a new, final "Catholic Orthodoxy" aimed at absorbing the Orthodox Churches and integrating them into its framework: something that is impossible anyhow.

Consequently, it has to be concluded that Uniatism is not a final solution, but merely an experiment of union. It is a passing stage for the Churches in transition which, once the union between Eastern Orthodoxy and Catholicism has been achieved, will have to reintegrate into Orthodoxy Churches of the corresponding rite.

This being so, we cannot understand how certain Uniate Churches, by becoming comfortable in their Uniatism as if their Church were a permanent institution, try to solve the gigantic conflict in their own manner and to their own advantage alone. We do not understand how they can judge beforehand the manner in which Latins and Orthodox would be willing to unite, by trying to immediately achieve a paradoxical "inter-uniate" union upon which the unity of Christianity must ultimately take place. They incessantly repeat: "We Eastern Catholics - all of us, irrespective of rite - should unite under one authority alone. In every country of the East (as well as all other Eastern Christians, no matter where they live), we Eastern Catholics -- Greeks, Copts, Slavs, Syrians, Armenians, Maronites, Chaldeans, Indians, etc. - we should unite under one head and in one jurisdiction, for in this way we will give the world a viable example of Christian unity."

I wonder who is filling their heads with such nonsense? Who is telling them that, for example, by subordinating the Greek Catholic hierarchy to the Coptic Catholic Patriarchate they will thereby inspire the Greek Orthodox hierarchy of the Patriarchate of Alexandria and of all Africa to decide to throw themselves into the arms of the Catholic Church? Who tells them that even by putting the Latin Catholic Church of Palestine under the Greek Catholic Patriarchate an uncontrollable urge to join the Catholic Church would suddenly overtake the Armenian Orthodox? Where do they get the idea that Latins and Greeks, Chalcedonians and non-Chalcedonians, etc. - to whom belongs the right to decide the day and the manner in which to unite - would accept such a simplistic formula as the one they recommended?

If we want Uniatism to become a model for future unity between Orthodoxy and Latin Catholicism it is necessary that Uniatism become a true reproduction of the Orthodox half of the Church. But in order to promote unity between the Greek Orthodox Patriarchate of Alexandria and the Catholic Church, should one simply dissolve the Greek Catholic Patriarchate into the Coptic Catholic Patriarchate? Such a proposal has no relation whatever to unity and between Greeks and Latins, chiefly being considered here. On the contrary, this proposal sins against authentic unity in two ways: a.) because unity is not to be defined as the *disappearance* of one Church in favor of another; b) because it is not directly the unity between the Coptic Orthodox Patriarchate and the Greek Orthodox Patriarchate in Alexandria

103

that should be attempted, but it is more important that each of them unite with the Catholic Church, and thus preserve their individual integrities. If then the producing of a local model for unity is desired in view of achieving it later on the Orthodox-Catholic scale, the attempt ought to be immediately made to achieve union between Catholic Copts and Orthodox Copts, Greek Catholics and Greek Orthodox, Syrian Catholics and Syrian Orthodox, etc. There being no union at present, a progressive shrinking of the chasm between Churches of the same rite and tradition has to be our immediate goal. I repeat what I have said countless times before: *In order that Uniatism may serve the cause of unity, it is necessary that every Uniate Church de-latinize itself by reassimilating all that is legitimate, authentic and apostolic in the corresponding Orthodox Church of its rite.* It is necessary that the Greek Catholic become religiously and ecclesiastically more Greek, the Catholic Copt become more Coptic, the Armenian Catholic become more Armenian, the Syrian Catholic become more Syrian, etc.

Any effort outside of this one or in opposition to it, would be sheer childishness (not to call it something worse!) and even an obstacle to Christian Unity because no Church or group of believers however humble it may be, should be compelled to accept union by assimilation or disappearance. It is simply unjust for anyone to expect this! Indeed, we envision the true unity of the distant future to include several different rites in which almost everyone can find a home: an Anglican Catholic rite, a Presbyterian Catholic rite, perhaps even a Jewish Catholic rite, and many, many more; with some of them even containing smaller subdivisions.

Although those who recommend the merging of all Uniate Catholic hierarchies consider this nothing more than a hierarchic union, it would really be much more, for it would deprive each Church of its patriarchate (and, as we have seen, the Patriarchate is the only genuine guardian of each Church's patrimony and one of the only checks on the spread of heterodoxy). Should this come about, it would leave each rite nothing except the liberty to celebrate liturgical services in its own manner, and would wrongly imply that "a Church consists only in the practice of a liturgical ritual." But even such a liturgical ritual, isolated from all else that constitutes its ecclesiastical rite, would eventually become a bastardized type of ritual for, cut off from its beginnings and deprived of the mother Church that should nurture it, the liturgical rite itself would deteriorate also.[11]

Such ideas, more nationalistic than religious, more separatist than Catholics, are opposed to ecumenism, whose fundamental principle is to realize unity in diversity, to unite without amalgamating, we should say, in the spirit and style of the ancient traditional Chalcedonians.

In any case, the role of Uniatism is not to superimpose its own solution upon the complex problem of disunity because, as we have said before, Uniatism is not itself one of the major parties to be united, and because Uniatism has already compromised itself in an experiment of union which has not succeeded in resolving the problem.

If, however, unity should involve some give and take, it would be up to the major parties immediately concerned (i.e. to the Latin Catholics and the Orthodox) to determine the time for union. Meanwhile, let us not be more concerned with uniting Uniates into one jurisdiction than with the uniting of divided Christians, nor let us to be too eager to reinforce and boost our own Uniatism at the expense of a lasting unity.

Postscript

By way of a postscript or appendix to this chapter, I quote an edited extract from an interview given to the Greek newspaper *Eleftheros Kosmos (Free Universe)* on November 30, 1970, by Cardinal Jan Willebrands, then president of the Roman Catholic Pontifical Secretariat for Promoting Christian Unity:

Question: "The Greek Orthodox Churches have often referred to the Uniate movement, saying that it is an obstacle to the genuine beginning of a dialogue aimed at the *rapprochement* of the two Churches. [What is your opinion?]"

Reply: "The fact of the Catholic and Orthodox Churches not being in full communion creates an abnormal situation between them, *a situation which is against nature*! Two Churches living by the same Christ, having the same Lord, cannot be divided between themselves. The scandal is all the more painful and becomes unbearable when this situation is found in the same locality, the same city, the same neighborhood; between Christians having the same culture, the same ecclesial tradition, the same way of praying and celebrating the liturgy. This is the case with the Eastern Catholic communities, whose existence and presence make one acutely aware of the scandal, that of the division of Christians.

"This awareness is not an obstacle to the re-establishment of unity but it should serve as a stimulus to put an end to the scandalous and unnatural situation of our division. The re-establishment of full communion is the only real and lasting solution. So long as we are divided, the Roman Catholic Church cannot refuse the request for communion addressed to her by individuals or communities because their conscience demands this of them, and because they are convinced that they are obeying the Holy Spirit. And this communion with the Roman Catholic Church does not demand in any case that the person or community in question should abandon the legitimate Christian traditions in which they have received or lived the Gospel. All the more reason why the Catholic Church does not demand that they abandon the Eastern traditions of which the Second Vatican Council said that they are "admirably rooted in Holy Scripture, fostered and given expression in liturgical life, and nourished by the living tradition of the Apostles and by the writings of the Apostles and by the writings of the Fathers and spiritual authors of the Christian Orient; they are directed towards a right ordering of life, indeed, towards a full contemplation of Christian truth." (*Unitatis Redintegratio*, 17.)

"These communities must not be looked upon as an attack upon, or a challenge to the Orthodox Church. They are *the inevitable consequence of an abnormal situation*, as well as of the respect due to the liberty enjoyed by every person or group to choose his ecclesial membership."[12]

Notes

1. Cf. Mark 1, 22.

2. It should be noted here that not only were Eastern Catholic hierarchies erected but that *Latin* Catholic Patriar-

chates of Constantinople, Alexandria, Antioch and Jerusalem were set up as rival claimants to the ancient Orthodox sees. It was during the last few years of his pontificate that Pope John XXIII, of happy memory, announced he would not name new patriarchs for the vacancies in the Latin Patriarchates of the East. Furthermore, he ordered the Latin Patriarchates of Constantinople, Alexandria and Antioch abolished, declaring that the Latin Patriarchate of Jerusalem would continue to exist for the present but would also be dissolved as soon as its throne becomes vacant. The number of irritants separating East and West would have been reduced if Pope Paul VI had followed this policy.

3. Here and elsewhere in this book we purposely use the word "Orthodox" in the sense of authentic Eastern tradition, the schism being regarded here as nothing more than an accident of history.

4. *Cleri Sanctitati* was promulgated by Pope Pius XII on June 2, 1957, though it was unfinished at that date. During Vatican II the "new" Code was shelved and another "newer" Code authorized, however, work had hardly begun on the "newer" Code at the time of [the original] publication of this book (1972).

5. Italics mine [E.Z.].

6. As Americans we might be surprised at Archbishop Zoghby's restrictive approach. After all, this canon allows traffic in both directions and we have gained many dedicated Eastern Catholics through transfer from the Latin rite. We must remember that in the Middle East, transfer of rite is generally a one way street carrying Easterners who culturally identify with Europe away from their own community. [F.S.]

7. Cf. all the Papal documents pertaining to the Christian East since the time of Leo XIII.

8. Is this not the impression given when, in 1991, Pope John Paul II established Roman Catholic jurisdictions in Russia staffed by Western missionaries while at the same time

asking Greek Catholics to moderate their activities in their own lands? [F.S.]

9. This is because the Latins have the financial influence that we do not have. cf. Archbishop Joseph Raya: "Difficulties Old and New," *Message of Galilee*, Vol. I, No. 1 (new series), 1969, pp. 6-7.

10. Is this not similar to the desire to merge the divergent Greek, Syriac, Coptic and other Eastern canonical traditions into a unified canon law for "the Eastern Church"? [F.S.]

11. We have already spoken of the anti-ecumenical character of the unification of Uniate Catholic hierarchies. We add here that this proposed unification is not feasible because of psychological, historical and practical reasons known to all who give it serious thought.

     If we want to be practical and to act in accordance with the mind of the Second Vatican Council, let us try rather to bring about a closer collaboration among the different hierarchies by holding national or regional assemblies of bishops more regularly.

12. The entire interview in English translation is in the Feb. 1971 issue of *Information Service,* the bulletin of the Secretariat for Promoting Christian Unity.

Ten - Uniatism and the Office of Patriarch

The patriarchal office is a traditional, conciliar and universal institution. From Christian antiquity the Ecumenical Councils have recognized the existence of Mother Churches which have spread the Christian faith throughout the world and given birth to other Churches. They conferred upon them the title of *patriarchates*. These founding Churches are Rome (universally primatial and Mother of the Western Churches), Constantinople (the "New Rome" - destined to see the seven great Ecumenical Councils in or near itself - which preached the Gospel in Russia and throughout Eastern Europe), Alexandria (Mother of the Churches of Africa and center of theological and monastic activity), Antioch (religious capital of Syria, with its Assyro-Chaldean, Indian and even Chinese offshoots) and Jerusalem ("Mother of all Churches" and cradle of Christianity).

These patriarchal Churches did not enjoy a mere ephemeral glory, only to give other Churches the trouble of supplanting them later on. Through the centuries and despite the vicissitudes of the times, they remained citadels of Christianity guarding the faith, the doctrine and the liturgical and monastic life whose foundations they had previously lain, cherishing and nurturing the Churches born of their apostolic activity.

Indeed after the ecclesiastical rupture between East and West, the East even bestowed the patriarchal title upon other important Churches such as Moscow and All Russia, Serbia, Rumania and Bulgaria. Extending the patriarchal title to these Churches, however, has not lessened the importance of the ancient founding Churches in the eyes of the Orthodox. Neither has the extending of the patriarchal title lessened the importance of the patriarchal institution itself. In fact, its very flexibility is a sign of its universality.

The opposite has been true in the Catholic Church. By making patriarchates of certain Uniate Churches and by heaping titles upon them, the Roman administrations have, in fact, *reduced* these Uniate patriarchates to the level of *suffragan* sees of the Latin Patriarchate of Rome! To be completely honest, is it not in the Congregation for the Eastern Churches in Rome that the headquarters of the Uniate Churches are to be found?[1]

The popes have often declared that the Eastern Catholic Churches were to retain all their rights and privileges but the Roman Curia, upon which the Popes have ever depended to help the Easterners safeguard their valuable traditions, have never had any sympathy whatever for the patriarchal form of ecclesiastical government. There are two explanations for this: 1. the true patriarchal concept has lain dormant in the West for such a long time that the Roman Church, for the past thousand years at least, has simply not been able to think in terms of a patriarchate; and 2. since the only authentic patriarch in the Western half of the Church was the Pope of Rome, the Western mind has not been able to disassociate the office of patriarch from the office of pope. A further reason is a pragmatic one: the powerful Roman Curia, not wishing to permit the Uniate Eastern Churches self-government for various reasons, has retained control of them despite the many papal pleas to the contrary.

Let me elucidate by turning back the pages of time. Leaning on the universal primacy of its diocesan bishop (i.e. the Pope), the clergy of Rome had already attributed to themselves the power to administer the whole Patriarchate of the West and intended to assume equally the responsibility for the whole Church of God. The pope, being simultaneously, but on *different* levels, Bishop of Rome, Primate of Italy, Patriarch of the West, and Pope of the Universal Church, it was thought that in order to exercise the different charges, he should be assisted by hierarchically distinct agencies capable of representing the episcopacy adequately on these various levels. I, too, believe that the Pope ought to be assisted by his local clergy for the administration of his diocese (Rome) and also perhaps of the suffragan dioceses of Italy whose primate he is, but the responsibilities of ruling the Latin Patriarchate of the West ought to be assumed by the Latin episcopate or their delegates near the Holy Roman See, assembled in Patriarchal Synod around the pope in the exercise of his powers as Patriarch of the West. Where the whole Church is concerned, the responsibility for its administration ought to fall upon the universal Catholic episcopate (or the representatives commissioned by them) to coordinate, under the world-wide primacy of the Pope, the life and activities of the entire Church.[2]

The Roman clergy have established themselves, with the pope and in his name, as administrators of the whole Catholic Church and thereby showing themselves to be in total disregard of the three different levels. This form of government has been strengthened and has resulted in the reduction of the episcopal powers of divine right. Initiated at the reform of Cluny in the tenth century and furthered by the Council of Trent, this form of government reached its climax after the First Vatican Council of the last century. All the Eastern Catholic Churches were placed under the tutelage of the Roman Curia. The Eastern Patriarchs, sole representatives within Catholicity of the traditional patriarchs who before the separation surrounded the Bishop of Rome and presided over the destinies of Christianity; these patriarchs to whom, *exclusively*, the newly elected Popes sent their profession of faith, these very same Uniate Eastern Patriarchs have been relegated to the background.

The actual order of priority (or precedence), minutely and scrupulously specified in the Canons 215-219 of the Code of Eastern Canon Law promulgated in Rome in 1957 and presented to the Uniate Churches (and through them to the whole of Orthodoxy with the expectation that it may serve as a pattern for unity!?) places the patriarchs, archbishops and bishops of the local Churches, *in their own territories*, after not only the Pope of Rome, but also the 100-plus Cardinals, the nuncios, internuncios and apostolic delegates even though they have not donned the bishops' purple.[3]

The Cardinals owe their position of priority not to the archiepiscopal or episcopal see they occupy (unless this see is in Italy and a suffragan of the Roman see) but to the title they received on the day of their investiture as cardinals, for this ceremony incorporated them into the Diocese of Rome, making them members of the local Roman clergy. (As an example, let's take the Archbishop of Lyons, France, the Primate of the Gauls. He does not owe his rank - a rank that makes him higher than most other bishops, archbishops and primates - to his Archdiocese of Lyons. He owes it to his Roman title and to the parish Church of Santissima Trinita al Monte Pincio, of which he became titular pastor on the day of his promotion to the Cardinalate. Suffice it to say that each Pontifical Year Book from Rome says: "The Cardinals, who originally were the parish priests of the twenty-five main Roman churches and the seven (later to be expanded to fourteen) regional deacons and the six palatine deacons, and the seven suburbicarian bishops, have become counsellors and cooperators of the Pope."

Here then, is the order of the sees in the Roman Catholic Church today: the Holy See of Rome, then follow all the churches disseminated throughout Italy including those in Rome, borne by the Cardinals. This makes us able to enumerate; after the see of Peter at Rome, the 100-plus sees of the Latin Cardinals before arriving at the Apostolic sees and the four patriarchates of Constantinople, Alexandria, Antioch and Jerusalem.

Titular Patriarchs *vs.* Residential Patriarchs

Even after the precedence of the Cardinals is assured,[4] the Eastern patriarchs are not assured a place in the hierarchy.

If the concern were only about precedence we would be facing a simple matter of ceremonial precedence - such as the seating of patriarchs and cardinals at future Ecumenical Councils, etc. - that could be easily solved. But the code explicitly states that the patriarchates of the East are now considered *suffragan* sees of the Diocese of Rome! When we consult the same code we see that the Eastern Catholic patriarchs, in whom have always been vested the highest authority within their own Churches (and within the Universal Church), now have as many theoretical powers as they always had, but that *they are prevented by the Roman Curia* from exercising them!

Before the advent of Uniatism, Orthodoxy could still hope to resume the dialogue initiated at the Council of Florence in 1439 when relations between Greek Orthodoxy and the Church of Rome were opened again. At that time, the Greeks demanded recognition of the millenarian right stating that the Eastern patriarchs were the first bishops of Christianity along with the Pope of Rome. The Roman Pope Eugene IV officially agreed to this petition. In contemporary times, would the Holy See of Rome be disposed to acknowledge this pre-eminence of the patriarchal institution in the Church? If the answer is no, I feel that the results of all well-intentioned dialogue with Orthodoxy will be doomed to failure.

Regretfully, the Uniate experience does not seem to indicate such an improved course of action. However, Vatican Council II by reviving, to some extent, the Catholic Church's estimation of the episcopate and by bestowing honor upon the national or regional episcopal assemblies, has prepared the way for a collegial form of government which, instead of fighting against the patriarchal institution, will spread its benefit to the entire Catholic Church. Despite the progress, the Uniate Churches should continue to contribute to the general effort of the episcopate by making the voice of the Christian East heard. The Greek Catholic Church which, within Catholicity, is the Eastern heir of Chalcedonian Orthodoxy and conscious of its solidarity with the quarter-billion Byzantine Orthodox; the Greek Catholic Church of the Byzantine rite has never endorsed or approved of the diminution of rights proper to the Uniate patriarchs because this sad situation deforms and humiliates the patriarchal institution. At the First Vatican Council, the Greek Catholic Patriarch Gregory Youssef fought against the tendency of Roman centralization and signed the acts of that Council only after having added these qualifying words: "[I sign this document] so long as its provisions do not infringe upon the legitimate rights and privileges of the Patriarchs."

A century later at the Second Vatican Council, the late Greek Catholic Patriarch Maximos IV, setting aside the weakness of his 85 years, raised his voice (described by several press reporters as "fiery") to affirm in similar terms the rights of the episcopate and those of the patriarchate.

Could there have been any more favorable occasion than the Second Vatican Council to give every Church its proper place in the universal Church and to revive the episcopacy and the patriarchate by again honoring the episcopal and patriarchal titles of the Pope of Rome (titles which he possesses as Bishop of Rome and as Patriarch of the West) on the basis of equality with his brothers the diocesan bishops and the Apostolic Patriarchs? I think that it would be hard to find a place where the Eastern Catholic Churches could have obtained more exposure.

Pope John XXIII of happy memory, understood ecclesiastical history very well. As soon as he was elected to the Papacy, he began reminding everyone that he was indeed Bishop of the City of Rome. He started out by getting acquainted with his city, visiting its people, examining the needs of the Romans, blessing, comforting and aiding them. The respect for a bishop and his pastoral duties was one of the reasons leading to the summoning of the Second Vatican Council. This Pope really believed in the episcopacy, in his own episcopacy, in its charisms, in the divine right of bishops to direct their own diocese and (in union with the pope) to assume the collective responsibility for governing the universal Church. He called them all together to share with them the charisms of their episcopate and to make it possible for them to participate in those of his own primacy.

Thanks to the healthy boost given the episcopacy by this late pope, the Fathers left the first session of the Council more aware of their dignity as bishops. The Eastern patriarchs did not desire more than this for themselves, because the patriarchate is equal to the episcopacy in its fullest sense. The patriarchal and synodal government is, indeed, the normal outcome of the collegial episcopal government. Derived from the latter, it protects it from excessive centralization.

The Uniate Eastern Churches have contributed to the success of the Council thanks, not only to the wise and forceful speeches and interventions of many of their leaders but also, and perhaps most of all, thanks to the fact of their very presence at the Council, for this led the assembly members to rethink the problem of Christian unity. Here are three important facts:

First of all, the presence of the Uniate Churches at the Council reminded the participants *in a very concrete way* of the existence of a Christian world different from the Latin milieu and stirred-up these Latin Fathers, making them face the facts of a diverse and a separated Christianity. This

Eastern presence helped them to get better acquainted with the other Christianity and enabled them to open themselves to a wider understanding of the whole of Christendom.

Secondly, the variety of prayers and liturgical ceremonies which were celebrated in the presence of the Conciliar Fathers, made the latter able to sample a tiny portion of the magnificent glories and riches of the East.

Thirdly, the Latin Council Fathers saw themselves compelled to explain the existence of this authentic form of Christianity within the Catholic Church. Further, they found that the Roman primacy does not confer the parenthood of all Churches on the Roman Church, but that the Latin-Roman Church is just another *local* Church.

Vatican Council II would certainly have gained more ecumenicity if the Orthodox patriarchs had been present. Also, the great numerical majority of the Latin Fathers would have been less overwhelming if the Uniate patriarchs of the East had not disappeared behind the Roman cardinalate. Was not the Western Church almost numerically nonexistent at the Great Ecumenical Councils?

Uniate Patriarchs Are Fathers of Their People

A few people would object that the Uniate patriarchs receive high honors that they are not entitled to. They base this objection on the fact that these patriarchs preside over such small numbers of faithful. Their opposition is sinful because a) these patriarchs are the sole representatives of Eastern Orthodoxy within Catholicism, and b) because the number of faithful has never been the most important factor in determining the Church's hierarchical structure. Just look at the Cardinal-President of the Fabric of Saint Peter.[5] How many "thousands" of faithful has he under his jurisdiction? And what about the Cardinal-Protector of the Vatican Library and his subjects? Well, neither have *any* subjects.

What of cardinals in mission countries, have they any more faithful than we? But although their communities be very young in Christianity, they have been placed *above* the men holding title to the Apostolic patriarchates! In short, numbers of faithful is not of prime importance and, consequently, this objection is valueless.[6]

Another objection that could arise in certain minds is: Since the institution of the cardinalate by the Holy See of Rome, the office of patriarch has become obsolete. Here is our answer: a) the popes never claimed to put an end to patriarchates by instituting the cardinalate. On the contrary, since the beginning of the Uniate movement they have proclaimed the dignity of the patriarchal institution and their desire to safeguard its rights and privileges; b) the popes are not in the habit of imposing laws and disciplinary measures in the non-Catholic Churches. In 1439, Pope Eugene IV declared[7] that cardinals should have the precedence over patriarchs, but *which* patriarchs were not mentioned. He could not have meant the Uniate patriarchates, for they did not yet exist.

Could it have been the Orthodox Patriarchs of Constantinople, Alexandria, Antioch or Jerusalem? We do not think so because the papal decision at the Florentine Council was to place the patriarchs directly below the pope, as had been the custom since ancient times, and it is inconceivable that *in the very same year* Pope Eugene would circumvent the conciliar decision. To say that such a decision justifies the priority of cardinals over patriarchs is to attribute to this pope a far too solemn violation of the given word or of the signed contract. Moreover, Orthodoxy never seemed to have worried much about this papal proclamation.

Whatever the fact and whatever the decision made by Pope Eugene IV, everyone knows that this could not bind the entire Church forever. We are living in ecumenical times, and we must focus on the future, while glancing back at the past in order to mend our human errors.

A third objection finds its origin in the recent past. The new Code of Eastern Canon Law confirms the priority Cardinals have over Patriarchs.[8] Following promulgation of this code, ecumenists asked themselves: In the mind of the Holy See at Rome, is this code binding only on the Uniate Churches or does it bind all other Christian Churches of the East as well? In other words, when the code speaks about the Eastern Churches does this refer only to the Uniates, or does the code mean both the Uniate and the Orthodox Churches combined? If the latter be correct, the effect would be to consider the Orthodox Church as ecclesiastically nonexistent and as having forever been replaced within the Catholic Church by Uniatism. Almost all of the popes during the past thousand years have discarded such a theory and so must we. Also, we have been assured by the last few popes that the Uniate patriarchs preside over their own faithful *alone* and not over the Orthodox who are separated from the Roman Catholic Church even though, at present, these patriarchs are the only Eastern representatives within Catholicism. Since this is now the case, we logically conclude that the present Code of Eastern Canon Law and all the measures concerning the Eastern Churches taking by the Holy See of Rome, are of interest only to the Uniates and are merely provisional. The Holy See declared almost as much when she permitted Vatican II's document on the Uniate Churches to be named: *Decretum de Ecclesiis Orientalibus* (*Decree On the Eastern Catholic Churches*).

At the time of reunion, new statutes on the relations between the Eastern Churches and the Latin Church will need to be redefined for, at that time, all will be within one and the same Church which will not be more Western than Eastern, not more Latin than Orthodox. Everything will have to be reexamined in the light of the traditions and decisions adopted by common agreement in the great Ecumenical Councils of the first millennium, for they preceded the separation.

Orthodoxy and the Roman Primacy

The doctrine of the Roman primacy has to be presented to the Orthodox within the framework of the Eastern tradition. It must be stressed that this doctrine is closely bound to the universal episcopate and is compatible with it. The primacy must be stripped of all its Roman, Latin and Western trappings so as to appear as a center of universal charity and focal point for unity, and not as a local Church or the religious offshoot in the East of an invading Western imperialism. The papacy should cease to be identified exclusively with the Diocese of Rome, the Western Church, the College of Cardinals, or with the Roman Curia. Peter was the first among the apostles. He and his successors should be looked up to, as they are the first among all bishops. The upper echelon of the Church is not composed of the Pope presiding over the College of Cardinals, nor the Pope acting through the Roman Curia. The highest ranks of the Church consists of the Pope presiding over the episcopate of the various local Churches or, to be more exact, it is made up of this episcopate presided over by the pope. This proves that nobody can supersede the bishops: no priest, be he a cardinal-priest; no deacon, be he a cardinal-deacon; no church dignitary without episcopal character, even though he is a nuncio or an apostolic delegate.

The cardinals or the members of the Roman Curia[9] can only be the pope's delegates to the pastoral episcopate and can therefore not put themselves in the place of the bishops or expropriate their powers. The pope, as universal primate, likewise has only the powers which his primacy confers upon him, *and no more*! He cannot, without legitimate motivation, gobble up any of the episcopal powers, because these powers are of divine right.

In the Christian East, the episcopate has as its agents, all members of itself and those chosen by it, the patriarchs. In his study on safeguarding the rights of the Eastern Church, the late Archbishop Peter K. Medawar, counsellor of the late Patriarch Maximos IV, enumerated the patriarchate's proper prerogatives:

"The patriarch," he writes, "is the most eminent guardian of the deposit of faith in the world. He has a major responsibility for its true and integral diffusion everywhere, but principally within his own jurisdiction. He watches over discipline, private and public morals in his territory; he is the official spokesman of his Church and of its peoples in all circumstances.

"In the Ecumenical Councils, the patriarchs of the Apostolic Sees occupy the first place, after the Bishop of Old Rome. In conformity with the ancient law, these patriarchs have the right and even the obligation to carry the burden of governing the Universal Church together with the Holy Father and to do so in a more outstanding and formal manner than the other bishops. More than once the Bishop of the ancient and venerable Rome has acknowledged these rights and obligations."[10]

Even Pope Gregory the Great wrote to one of the patriarchs that Saint Peter, who founded the Apostolic

Patriarchal Sees of Rome and Antioch, still occupies them both himself in the person of those who succeed him in these sees.[11]

Notes

1. In 1965, the Eastern Catholic patriarchs were named associate members of the Congregation for the Eastern Churches. Yet this does not attenuate this fact but, on the contrary, confirms it. In this Roman dicastery which presides over the destiny of "dioceses, bishops, clerics, religious and faithful of the Eastern rites", there are 30 Western rite cardinals. What would anyone think of a commission in charge of the administration of the Archdiocese of New York composed of Eastern patriarchs as full-fledged members with the actual archbishop of that metropolis only an associate member with little more than advisory powers? Yet this is exactly the situation in which all the Uniate Eastern Catholic Churches find themselves today! See Chapter Eleven, below.

2. The Roman Synod, whose first meeting was held in 1967, is really not a Synod at all, for it lacks any decision- making power.

3. More than once it has been said that we persist in the matter of precedence as if this were of utmost importance. However, it is the Eastern Code of Canon Law itself, made in Rome, that gives it such importance. The Code insists upon it so strongly yet with a finesse that hurts our feelings and arouses our suspicions. Two hypotheses that may account for the reason why the Code dwells so much on precedence are: 1.) because it attaches an intrinsic importance to it, in which case we, bishops of the Eastern rites, should not be blamed for insisting upon it, or 2.) because, by means of this precedence the Code aims to maintain privileged agencies in the Church (by this we mean the Roman Curia) which would reserve to themselves the right to govern all the Churches. In this case, our Eastern bishops and pastors would have the duty to carefully watch these ceremonial

regulations so as to recover our place in the universal Church. (*Again, Archbishop Zoghby is speaking about the aborted canons of 1957.*)

4. In response to protests such as that of Archbishop Zoghby, the Vatican's 1990 Code of Eastern Canon Law recognized again the conciliar order of precedence for the historic patriarchates, as follows:
"Can. 58 - Patriarchs of Eastern Churches precede all bishops of any degree everywhere in the world, with due regard for special norms of precedence established by the Roman Pontiff.
"Can. 59 - ...#2 The order of precedence among the ancient patriarchal sees of the Eastern Churches is that the first place comes to the see of Constantinople, after that Alexandria, then Antioch and Jerusalem.
"... #4 Among the patriarchs of the Eastern Churches who each are of the same title but who preside over different patriarchal Churches, he has precedence who was first promoted to the patriarchal dignity."[F.S.]

5. This Vatican agency has the janitorial care of Saint Peter's Basilica alone, and has a cardinal as its head.

6. To illustrate the importance of Patriarchs to the Christian East, we refer the reader to the interview of Archpriest Vitali Borovoy, one of the Moscow Orthodox Patriarchate's official observers at the Second Vatican Council, by Miss Maria Jung. It also appears in this book in the chapter "The 'Promotion' of Patriarchs."

7. In the Bull *Non Mediocre*.

8. Again, Archbishop Zoghby is speaking about the aborted canons of 1957. See Note 4, above. [F.S.]

9. We would be unfair to the College of Cardinals if we were to say that the Roman centralization was intended for their own benefit alone. In fact, although the members of the College of Cardinals receive great honors and have a higher rank than other ecclesiastical dignitaries, only those who are members of the Curia enjoy any real authority. The only

notable power common to all cardinals is the duty to take part in the election of the pope. This privilege gives them special honor in the eyes of the world. Also, the exceptional glory that has surrounded the person of the pope since Vatican Council I, has undoubtedly enhanced the prestige of the cardinals, his assistants.

But once the pope is elected and enthroned, the cardinals not staying behind in a curial post return home and resume their former position and duties, exercising their pastoral function and obeying the same government as the other residential bishops. As to all the other bishops (including the cardinals), the Roman congregations send them the instructions and directives that have to be observed in the administration of their dioceses. Have they not sometimes been surprized to see important matters pertaining to their own jurisdictions become the object of ready-made decisions prepared by Roman Dicasteries without their collaboration and even without their knowledge?

The Roman Curia needs drastic reform - more than the token reforms made after Vatican II - or it should be abolished, the powers being completely returned to the episcopate from whom they have been taken over the past thousand years.

10. Cf. "The Rights of the Eastern Church" by Archbishop Medawar in *The Eastern Churches and Catholic Unity*, ed. Patriarch Maximos IV Sayegh (New York, Herder and Herder, 1963, pp. 132-157.)

11. Patrologia Latina 77, 890-891, "Letter of Pope Gregory I of Rome to Patriarch Eulogios of Alexandria".

Eleven - The "Promotion" of Patriarchs

Patriarchs can be promoted! - at least in the Catholic Church they can! In fact, they received their most recent promotion in 1965; and commentaries and editorials in the Church press encouraged us to rejoice at the event. The official enthusiasm, however, had a kind of false heartiness about it. What the "promotion" involved was this: the Eastern Patriarchs had been made *associate* members of the Congregation for the Eastern Churches. In the usual Roman manner, this Congregation supervises the various "Uniates", i.e. those sections of the Eastern Church which have entered into communion with Rome over the past several centuries. When those "unions" were achieved Rome promised, and continually promises, to honor and preserve "all the rights and privileges" of these Eastern Catholic Uniate Churches. Before this "promotion", Their Beatitudes, the Eastern Catholic Patriarchs, held no positions in the Congregation; now, they are involved - or should we say entangled? The Eastern Patriarchs now serve as "coadjutors" to the thirty Latin Cardinals[1], for the latter are the only official and real members of the Oriental Congregation. But it is only in this one area that the Patriarchs will be the equals of the Latin Cardinals, and of the Latin Patriarch of Jerusalem (who traces his beginnings back to the time of the Crusades and has no claim to apostolic succession or to any patriarchal jurisdiction[2]. As far as the Roman Curia is concerned, this lone Latin Patriarch is their colleague.

What has been the reaction of Eastern Catholics to this so-called "promotion"? Courtesy demands that they be grateful; and, of course, they are! No doubt, with an outlook inherited from the Crusades and Pope Innocent III, the Curia could only have thought that it was doing the Patriarchs an honor and a favor in recommending them to membership in both the Curia and in the college of Cardinals. But in this post Conciliar era, in these days of *aggiornamento*, we cannot remain silent: we must be honest and plain-spoken. For its part, the Greek Catholic

122

Patriarchate [of Antioch] has made it clear, repeatedly and publicly, that it would be willing to tolerate many things to serve the cause of unity in our day, but that it cannot recognize the preference shown to Cardinals or the existence of a Latin Patriarchate in Jerusalem just as it could not be happy with the Latin Patriarchates of Constantinople. Alexandria or Antioch when they existed. For this reason, however beneficial the "honor" may appear, it is really only another bitter pill for Easterners to swallow.

Furthermore, besides the cause of unity in our own day and age, we must consider the unity of *yesterday*.... and that of *tomorrow*.

In times past, there were patriarchal rights and privileges whose preservation the Holy Roman See has solemnly assured with repeated promises. These rights and privileges surpass any authority of dignity which the Cardinals possessed in the past or which they now enjoy. There can be nothing less in the future. The Second Vatican Council turned to that future with the purpose of uniting all Christians, particularly hoping to unite Eastern Orthodoxy and Roman Catholicism. Since the Council possessed supreme and sovereign authority,[3] it would have been an unforgivable crime for its Eastern Fathers to neglect to enlighten its members as much as possible. We Easterners were called upon to reveal to the Council Fathers our own love for the Church. We proved that we believe in its Spirit-given wisdom which goes beyond mere human cleverness. Dutifully, and with great enthusiasm, we asked the Council to restore - in theory as well as in practice - all the rights and privileges we hold dear and which, over the course of the many years of union, the Curia has managed to take away from us a little at a time.

Perhaps the most illuminating comment on this situation took place at a dinner held in Rome during the Second Vatican Council. The incident involved Orthodox Archpriest Vitali Borovoy, one of the pair of observers sent to the Council by the Moscow Patriarchate.[4]

"At the dinner [in Rome] a German reporter, Miss Maria Jung, stationed in Rome, turned to the Russian Archpriest, with a question: 'Why didn't Patriarch Alexei put in an appearance when Monsignor Willebrands was in Moscow?[5]'

"'The Patriarch was at his summer residence in Odessa, Ukraine,' the Russian answered. 'Why should he have bothered to come to Moscow? After all, Monsignor Willebrands[6] is a mere prelate, like my colleague and myself [and not even a bishop].'

"'I see,' said the reporter. 'So if Cardinal Bea[7] himself had come, then the Patriarch would have gone to see him,' she said confidently.

"But the archpriest replied, 'I don't think that even a Cardinal would have been enough. A Cardinal is nothing more than a bishop.[8] A Patriarch is much more ... '"[9]

And so, we find that the negative reaction of the whole Orthodox Church to this "promotion" (whereby the Catholic Patriarchs of the East become the mere associates of the thirty Latin Cardinals on a Papal bureau which originally usurped the powers of those same Patriarchs and which today governs the Eastern Catholic Churches in the Patriarchs' stead) is justifiable. Indeed, what status do these Patriarchs now posses in the eyes of the Orthodox? Supposedly, they are the equals of their Orthodox counterparts in Constantinople, Alexandria, Antioch and Jerusalem or, at least, to the recent Patriarchates (Russian, Rumania, Bulgaria, Serbia, etc.). The "promotion" only makes them more "Roman".[10] Patriarchs are the dignity and the pride and joy of the Orthodox Church and her hierarchy. But Rome honors her own Eastern Catholic Patriarchs with hesitation and half-steps, with parsimony and "prudence", tempting them with "bribes" (such as the Cardinalate) and placebos, when what is really required is recognition and love and proper respect. Rome forever promises her Eastern Patriarchs these things but she doesn't see to it that her promises are kept, and that is the only real problem![11]

Notes

1. Among the thirty are two Eastern Cardinals, but they are incardinated into the diocese of Rome through the devise of titular churches, the real source of their dignity and position in the Curia.
2. It is only this formality which gives them any equal standing. At the sessions of the Second Vatican Council,

The "Promotion" of Patriarchs

they were indistinguishable from mere bishops and archbishops; their seating was covered with the same green velvet that covered the places of the 2500 other bishops and prelates. On the other hand, the Cardinals stood out in their seating and scarlet robes to match: eighty *patres conscripti* of the" Senate" of the Roman Church.

3. With the Pope playing the proper role, of course.

4. The report quoted here appeared in *The Catholic World*, New York, January 1963; and also in the March 15, 1963 issue of *Les Informations Catholiques* from Paris.

5. The Monsignor was in Moscow to make arrangements for the Russian Orthodox observers attend the Council.

6. He directs the Vatican's Secretariat for Promoting of Christian Unity and is now a Cardinal.

7. Bea is the former head of the Christian Unity Secretariat. A Jesuit, he had been the confessor to Pope Pius XII and was the biblical scholar who is said to have authored the encyclical on holy Scripture, *Divino Afflante Spiritu*. Made a Cardinal by Pope John XXIII, he was a progressive at the Council. He died in December, 1967 and was replaced by his assistant, Cardinal Willebrands.

8. Pope John XXIII's move to ordain to the episcopacy all cardinals who were not bishops was laudable but, practically, it only served to bolster the power of the Roman Curia, for only among its own members had there been Cardinal-priests and Cardinal-deacons.

9. Any Orthodox clergyman or knowledgeable layman would have echoed the same sentiment; Eastern Catholics can do no less.

10. For the strict Roman canonists - of whom there are still quite a few - the Orthodox hierarchy doesn't even exist! Any realistic canonist would not see it this way nor would any of the Roman Pontiffs as is evidenced in those encyclicals where they promise to allow all of the Eastern traditions, etc., to remain intact. How could the Church, through the Popes, promise to conserve these rights and privileges if the hierarchy does not exist?

11. Writing elsewhere on the nomination of several Eastern Catholic patriarchs to the cardinalate by Paul VI, Archbishop Zoghby said, "The Catholic Patriarchs of the East can be promoted to the Cardinalate only because they are not true Patriarchs. ... For a Catholic Patriarch to be

named Cardinal and for that nomination to be considered a promotion, it is above all important that the patriarchal title be authoritatively redefined for Catholic ecclesiology. Yet, since the traditional patriarchal institution is still held in high esteem by the Orthodox Churches, it would be disrespectful for Catholics to use the patriarchal title in a diminished sense, just as it would be unethical for non-Catholics to use the title of Cardinal to designate members of their Patriarch's household and entourage." [F.S.]

Twelve - The Future of the Uniate Eastern Catholic Churches

The following chapter consists of an interview with Greek Orthodox Archbishop Chrysostom (Konstantinidis), Metropolitan of Myra and counsellor to the Ecumenical Patriarch Athenagoras I, followed by a response by Archbishop Elias Zoghby.

The first topic addressed concerns the question raised in Chapter Nine, of reintegrating the Eastern Catholic Churches into Orthodoxy.

Archbishop Chrysostom: First of all, I must emphasize that the concept of a "return" does not exist in Orthodox ecclesiology. There can never be any question then of our Uniate brothers "returning" to Orthodoxy, even less of being *forced* to "switch" to Orthodoxy, as unfortunately happened in certain countries following the Second World War. What must be found though, is the best possible way to incorporate them into Orthodoxy, their Church of origin. In the process, every precaution must be taken to respect the integrity of their ecclesiology, on one hand, and on the other, precautions must be taken to respect their own historical, national and ontological existence.

"The Eastern Uniates must be helped, by both Orthodoxy and Rome, in finding a solution to this problem of where they rightfully belong. They have so great a common heritage with the world of Orthodoxy, with whom they generally live side by side, that is really a duty for the Orthodox to be of assistance to them in this, just as it is for the Church of Rome with whom they have rather formal and "neo-historical" bonds, if I may be allowed such a term. But again I stress the necessity of this taking place without prejudice to them in any way whatsoever."

Question: What do you expect on the part of the Vatican on this subject?

Archbishop Chrysostom: "If the Catholic Church accepts on its agenda of matters for discussion the problem of the Byzantine Churches united to Rome, and if we meet around a table to study this question for the purpose of finding a solution, this in itself will be the beginning of a promising dialogue.[1] At the same time, it would be a gesture that Orthodoxy would deeply appreciate. "Let me make myself clear: I do not mean that the Vatican should commit itself to work for the abolition of what took place centuries ago and which today constitutes an ecclesial and ecclesiastical reality. I only say that we will view it as a concrete expression of good will if the Vatican agrees to discuss the Uniate problem, for it is a problem to both East and West, and one of the thorniest in our relations."

Question: What role do you think the representatives of these Uniate Churches ought to have in the discussions pertaining to their future?

Archbishop Chrysostom: "The representatives of these Churches must certainly have a voice and their voice must be heard. But, in my opinion, they ought not to participate directly in these discussions. Of course they must express their ideas, and Rome must be duly informed of their opinions and then, inform us of its own position on the question of the existence of the Eastern Catholic Churches.

"This question then, ought to be decided directly between the Roman Catholics and the Orthodox. The reasons for this are historical, canonical and even ecclesiological. The historical reasons are that it is Rome who created the Uniate Churches. The canonical reasons are that there exists only one Roman Catholic Church, in which co-exist many different rites, and it is with this Church that Orthodoxy will negotiate. Lastly, the ecclesiological reasons are that, in my opinion, it is the Roman Church herself who must remain faithful to her own ecclesiology which admits the principle that the Church of Christ may take on several different forms yet still remain one single institution.

"Our Eastern Catholic brothers who belong to the Eastern world and the Orthodox Church at least by their mentality, their traditions and their inner attitudes, possess incontestably precious values helpful, nay indispensable, to the East. They will certainly be able to enrich our Church but obviously only after some positive solution has been found to the puzzling question of 'Uniatism'."

Question: As it now stands, the question does not admit of any easy solution, does it?

Archbishop Chrysostom: "You are correct in your assumption. I personally feel that dialogue on that subject between Orthodox and Catholics is going to have its ups and downs, plus many a stalemate. But the very fact that we are now able to engage in discussion of our problems, many of which appear to be insoluble, indicates the metaphysical significance of the dialogue. Presently, we are beginning to work on questions which lead only, at this time, into blind alleys.

"If I have spoken here of the Churches united with Rome, it was only to give an example of the sort of problem we face in this post-conciliar era and which will perhaps shock the interested parties. But it is precisely for this reason, and to avoid creating any *a priori* obstacles for the dialogue, that I recommend a period of *pre-dialogue*. First, I would like to see something like a dialogue of exploration and exchange. Its job would be to set up the agenda for the actual dialogue, covering the pastoral, theological and social issues.

"I believe that this pre-dialogue can begin immediately since an ecumenical commission where we can freely express ourselves (I speak from experience) and seek together, satisfactory formulae and definitions; a commission of this nature has already been established. The first in centuries, this commission has given solid grounds for hope. It has demonstrated that there is a meeting of minds between Catholicism and Orthodoxy - the mutual lifting of anathemas is one proof of good will - completely destroying the theory holding that the two Churches cannot agree on anything.

"This is why I am optimistic about a solution of the problem of the Byzantine Churches united with Rome."

* * *

A Voice from the Byzantine East

Response

by Archbishop Elias Zoghby

I agree wholeheartedly with the statements of His Eminence, Archbishop Chrysostom, concerning the problem of the Byzantine Churches united with Rome. Yet I do not think that we should exaggerate the difficulties that will result. I don't think that they will be "at first sight insoluble" or that they "lead only into blind alleys."

As an Eastern Christian bishop of the Byzantine rite united with the See of Rome, I should scarcely like to believe that the existence of the Uniate Churches will present serious difficulties once the Catholic Church and Orthodoxy have resolved the other problems dividing them. It seems to me that the Uniate Churches would constitute a serious problem only if the Roman Church, after being reconciled with Orthodoxy, tried to keep us separated from our Churches of origin and thus make of us some sort of perpetual "schismatics".

The Orthodox Churches have the right and the duty to bring us back into the fold of Orthodoxy after reunion. But they cannot require the effective and immediate liquidation of our Churches as a condition for engaging in dialogue with the Catholic Church. Such a condition on their part would constitute a devious refusal to dialogue. Our Uniate Churches, which have existed for centuries, cannot disappear into thin air. And how else could they be dissolved except by absorption into the Latin Church? No one could conscientiously advise the latter. The only other alternative would be a return of the Uniates to Orthodoxy forthwith. But this is problematic in that the people, together with most of their bishops, would find themselves unprepared for such a premature and forced union, especially since their only reason for existence (as Uniates) is to aid the Roman Church, pushing it toward reconciliation with Orthodoxy.

If there be any fears that we Uniates may be incapable of readapting ourselves completely to Orthodoxy after unity is accomplished, let me quiet those apprehensions. There would certainly be cause for such fears if we were to return to Orthodoxy today, but union will take many years and the people on all sides will be psychologically prepared to accept it. Living in communion with the Roman-Latin Church as we do, and consequently depending upon it in large measure, we would [after union] experience a parallel maturation which would prepare us for reintegration into the reunited Church. Since our union with the Roman Church we have had to adapt ourselves, in some measure, to many things in Latinity quite foreign to us. We did not make these things our own but merely learned to co-exist with them. With Orthodoxy, however, we need not co-exist but merely to reintegrate ourselves into its life. Since we already live side-by-side with the Latins - and that is often a great penance - it would be quite easy for us to incorporate ourselves into Orthodoxy, our Mother.

We are in perfect accord with Archbishop Chrysostom's declaration that the dialogue must take place between the Roman and Orthodox Churches alone. After all, it is between these sister-Churches that the conflict exists; it is they whom the Schism separated. The Eastern Catholic Uniate Churches, of no matter which rite, cannot expect to take part in this dialogue as a partner. We cannot sit *vis-a-vis* the Latins because we have been affiliated with their Church in some manner and we owe some of what we are to them. Two of these things are: our western culture, both religious and profane; and our ecclesiology, incontestably a certain prolongation of Latin ecclesiology in the East.

The Uniate bodies cannot dialogue on an equal plane with Orthodoxy either, for we cannot offer Orthodoxy a Latin tradition because we are not Latins, nor can we offer it our own experience as Uniates. We would be foolish to ask them to accept our own *modus vivendi* in the Catholic Church as a status they might enjoy after union.

When we united ourselves with Rome, we did not attempt to solve any of the problems dividing East and West. After all the years since our union with Rome, i.e. since our establish as Uniate Churches, the issues dividing Rome and Orthodoxy are still the same. I repeat: these two Churches will, therefore, come together *without* the Uniates' involvement as equal participants.

His Eminence, Archbishop Chrysostom, admitted that he was impressed with our Uniate Churches and our bishops at the Second Vatican Council, and he declared:

A Voice from the Byzantine East

"Our Eastern Catholic brethren who belong to the Eastern world and the Orthodox Church at least by their mentality, their traditions and their inner attitudes, possess incontestably precious values helpful, nay indispensable, to the East."

In another place he says: "The representatives of these Churches must certainly have a voice and their voice must be heard. But, in my opinion, they ought not participate directly in these discussions. Of course, they must express their ideas, and Rome must be duly informed of their opinions and then, in turn, inform us of her own position [i.e., Rome's position] on the question of the existence of the Eastern Catholic Churches."

After union, the mode of existence of the Uniate Churches will be exactly as outlined in my remarks above.

As for our role in the dialogue to the reunification of East and West, again I agree with Archbishop Chrysostom *in toto*. The Uniates have a voice to be heard and a role to fulfill. This role, which began when Catholic-Orthodox dialogue was non-existent and even impossible, will lose importance as the direct dialogue grows.

In what ways then, have we carried out this role? First: After centuries of separation, when the Christian East and West lived in mutual ignorance and indifference, this Great Schism between them almost ceased to worry both sides. Each Church lived in its own world, self-sufficient and believing itself to be the one true Church of Jesus Christ. Even though the creation of the Uniate Churches - in most places dwelling side-by-side with Orthodoxy - must have been interpreted by the Orthodox as an act of hostility and defiance, this creation did, nonetheless, bring to mind the problem of reunion. Even the very un-ecumenical way in which the Uniate Churches were created began to evoke thought on both sides. We became "a sign of contradiction". Surely this is not the only instance where provocation, having overcome indifference, helped to initiate dialogue.

Even in the absence of dialogue, a real contact had been made between Catholics and Orthodox - forced upon both sides by the Uniate question - putting an end to their indifference. If our existence was, and still is, a cause for hostility between the Latins and the Orthodox, we must ever bear in mind that it does stimulate them to action.

Secondly: Since it is true that our Churches were united to the See of Rome without having first solved any of the disputed questions, it is also true that since our union, and above all recently, we have not ceased our harassment of Rome for a permanent solution. Obviously we have not always succeeded in imparting our views, but we have the satisfaction of knowing that we have played our part in preparing the Christian West for the opening up to the East now taking place. Thanks to our two Melkite Patriarchs, Maximos IV (+1967) and Maximos V and their predecessors, as well as to the Synod of Melkite Bishops, to many theologians sympathetic to our cause and to our many friends everywhere, the Roman Church today has in its hands rich documentation on all the problems concerning Eastern Christianity, its law, traditions, ecclesiology, liturgy, its dynamics and its very essence. Were a Catholic commission to make an exhaustive study of this documentation, it would provide the Roman See with the solution to many of the problems pertinent to the dialogue. We, the Uniate Catholics in communion with Rome, do not pretend to have solved all the problems, but can it be denied that an experiment such as we represent, even though unsuccessful, is rich in lessons?

Thirdly: What our Churches accomplished at the Council has already borne some fruit. We have given ample proof that the Eastern Uniate Churches, in spite of their inevitable weaknesses, were able to begin a dialogue with the Latins during the Second Vatican Council, the type of which the Orthodox are not yet able to have. Patriarch Athenagoras, *primus inter pares* of World Orthodoxy, acknowledged this when he declared to our late Patriarch Maximos IV: "You speak, at the Council, in our name."

Fourthly: It would be absurd for us, who acutely realize the limits and inherent weaknesses of Uniatism, to claim exclusive credit for the great accomplishments of the recent past. Yet was it not one of our hierarchs, Archbishop Peter K. Medawar, who suggested to the Bishop of Rome, fifteen years before Vatican II, to leave the confines of the Vatican and journey in person to meet the Orthodox Patriarch of Constantinople as brother to brother?[2]

Was is not our Melkite Synod and our Patriarch who petitioned Pope John XXIII to create a permanent organ in

Rome for the purpose of strengthening relations with the non-Catholic Christian Churches; an organ independent of the Holy Office (recently renamed: "The Sacred Congregation for the Doctrine of the Faith"), which could have exclusive jurisdiction over individuals or bodies who would seek to join the Catholic Church?[3] Was it not our Patriarch Maximos IV, of happy memory, who proposed the institution of a *Permanent* Synod of Bishops? Patriarch Maximos envisioned this synod's home to be in Rome. He also desired to see its members elected by the national (or regional) Episcopal Conferences, According to him, the permanent or quasi-permanent synod would be entrusted with the task of sharing with the pope the concerns of the universal Church.

To elaborate on this, let me quote the late Archimandrite Orestes Kerame, the chief theological consultant of the departed Patriarch Maximos IV. This excerpt is from an article published in 1960 and clearly demonstrates the doctrinal and pastoral concern of our late Patriarch.

"The Church is not entrusted to the pope alone but to the whole body of bishops merely presided over by the successor of Saint Peter, for the pope is but the *visible* head of the whole.

"Formerly, it was common to speak of the 'Pentarchy' by which was meant the Church governed by the Pope of Rome and the four Eastern patriarchs. Inasmuch as this theory did not deny the primacy of the pope it was, for its times, an indication of the truly catholic way of thinking. The five patriarchs, answerable for their bishops and in close contact with them, could well have prefigured a sort of permanent "Summit Council". A laudable plan, but we posit a greater number of hierarchs being entrusted with the actual day-to-day ruling of the re-united Catholic-Orthodox Church, for the Church is to be governed benevolently, and what better way of assuring this than by multiplying those in authority? I also feel that the patriarchs would care for the important matters in their Churches and, occasionally, advise the Holy Father in Rome. However, the Pope of Rome would preside over his Permanent Synod, as well as over the whole Church, as an "elder" and as a loving father.

"After all, just what is the Pope of Rome? Is not Peter, first of all, present in the Apostolic College, or on the contrary, is he the head, the president and "representative" of the local clergy of Rome? Obviously, no matter how honorable the condition of the primatial clergy of Rome, and no matter how normal its concurrence in the service of the ecumenical pope may be, among his co-responsible brethren it is the pope himself who is Peter."

To our credit also, and at the risk of sounding immodest, I must point out that the Synod of Melkite Bishops met in Cairo in 1958 to energetically oppose certain aspects of the Canon Law that had been promulgated by the Roman Church for all Eastern Catholics, i.e. the Uniates, or, those Easterners in visible communion with Rome. That Canon Law, in its chapter entitled "De Personis", was prejudicial to the rights and to the dignity of the Eastern Churches. This synod represented a high point in our Church's struggle to restore patriarchal synods, together with their powers, to the Catholic Church.

Fifth: At the Council and even before it, we were able to put the Latins in contact with an authentic non-Latin Christianity they scarcely knew. Afforded these opportunities we were able to prove to the Orthodox that even though we are a tiny minority in the Church dominated by an overwhelming majority of Latins, we were nonetheless capable of making our voice - their voice - heard. Reacting to this, the greater number of Council Fathers rallied to many of our ideas. We have thus proven to the Orthodox that a dialogue *between equals* has unlimited chances of success.

Now that direct contact between the Latins and the Orthodox has been established, we can do nothing but rejoice and leave to Orthodoxy the task of restoring unity.

To the Orthodox, and particularly to Archbishop Chrysostom, I say: You are at home in Orthodoxy; the Latins are at home in their Church: but we are *nowhere* at home! Even though we remain within the pale of the Roman Church we cannot feel at home in Catholicity because, as the Ukrainian Archbishop Joseph Slipyi so aptly remarked, "because Catholicity cannot be truly "Catholic" - universal - without *you*, without the other authentic and apostolic "half" of Christ's Church: Orthodoxy. We have no notion of replacing you in this [Roman Catholic] Church, for you are the only one capable of preparing for us [Uniates] a place in it. Only as the Catholic Church opens and affords you a loving home within its fold, on an equal basis with the Latins, will we be able to feel at home in it ourselves."

In the last analysis though, it is not you, or the Latins, or us who are most intimately involved; it is Jesus Christ. Can we indeed say that He has "a place to rest His weary head" as long as His Church is divided? Here we find the source and origin of the "divine" anguish of Athenagoras I, John XXIII and Paul VI.

As Eastern Uniates we can only pray, suffer, and render whatever service possible to assist in realizing our great desire, the union of the Christian East and West. We pray that Orthodoxy and Latin Catholicism, which are so far apart yet so close together, will soon reconstitute the "home" where Christ Jesus will be able to "rest His head" and where we too, after everyone else is settled, can find a humble place.

Notes

1. This question was placed at the head of the agenda for the Joint International Commission for Theological Dialogue between the Roman Catholic Church and the Orthodox Church at its Sixth Plenary Session, meeting June 6-15, 1990 in Freising, Germany, precipitated by the re-emergence of Greek Catholic Churches in the formerly Communist nations of Eastern Europe. The Commission issued a statement disclaiming Uniatism as follows:

"6b - The Term 'Uniatism' indicates here the effort which aims to bring about the unity of the Church by separating from the Orthodox Church communities of Orthodox faithful without taking into account that, according to ecclesiology, the Orthodox Church is a sister-church which itself offers the means of grace and salvation. In this sense and with reference to the document issued by the Vienna sub-commission, we reject 'Uniatism' as a means of unity opposed to the common Tradition of our Churches."

The subcommittee charged with continuing work on this issue in preparation for the 1992 Plenary Session notes the following: "Some important questions are still to be resolved. When they shall have been resolved, the Catholic Church and the Orthodox Church will have full communion, and by this very fact the difficulties caused by the Eastern Catholic Churches for the Orthodox Church will finally be uprooted." [F.S.]

2. The late Melkite Greek Catholic Archbishop Peter K. Medawar, Auxiliary to the late Patriarch Maximos IV, gave his views on this matter in his article: "Reflections on the Union of Churches," in *The Eastern Churches and Catholic Unity*, ed. Patriarch Maximos IV Sayegh (New York: Herder and Herder, 1963, p. 104 ff.).

3. This has been partially realized with the establishment of the Secretariat (now Council) for Promoting Christian Unity.

Part V - The Episcopate

Thirteen - Bishops and the Roman Primacy

Many Eastern Catholics, together with ecumenical experts and genuinely concerned people, still wonder why the Second Vatican Council (1962-1965) found it necessary to issue a separate document on the Eastern Catholic Churches united with Rome. Informed people everywhere see this move as an attempt to classify the Catholic Eastern rites as groups that form a sort of appendix to the universal Catholic Church. In saying this I am only stating a fact which is rather eloquently illustrated by another fact, namely that the Eastern Catholic bishops were present *within* that assembly and did neither constitute nor set up a separate ecumenical council outside of it. And, they spoke on all subjects, not merely those topics related to them or to their Churches. Furthermore, they formed (and still form) part of the entire, world-wide Catholic episcopate; they are not a body outside of it.

The Constitution on the Church (*Lumen Gentium*) would perhaps be more useful to everyone if it had been inspired to a greater degree by the traditions of both the Eastern and Western Churches - but particularly the Eastern - whose ecclesiologies complement each other so well. The patrimony of the Eastern Churches is very rich and constitutes by far the most important heritage of Christianity. Both parts of the Universal Church lived at peace and in harmony during the first ten centuries of our era. Yes, for the first thousand years of Christian history both Eastern and Western Christendom so existed, each having its own authentic theology, discipline, customs, spirituality, liturgical practices and usages, etc.; in short, its own true identity. Their separation, which seems to have been finalized only during the past two or three centuries, is an abnormal state of affairs. Therefore, it would have been helpful to the cause of reunion had the Council at least prefaced *Lumen Gentium* with a few paragraphs on the two particular Churches and mentalities. So we deeply regret that this document was issued with hardly even the slightest bit of Eastern flavoring inserted into it.

The Eastern Christian Churches have never denied the Roman primacy but have always considered it as a principle of Catholicity (which is one of the four marks of the true Church). However, during the centuries following the separation, this doctrine evolved to such a great extent in the Roman Church in a unilateral direction that it is scarcely recognized today by our Orthodox brethren. Formerly, the Roman Church rarely exercised its primacy over the Eastern Churches. This is a fact of great importance which we must bear in mind if we wish to have a just and fruitful dialogue with the Eastern Churches separated from the Church of Rome.

Each time *Lumen Gentium* speaks of the authority of bishops, it immediately subordinates it to that of the Roman Pontiff. This affirmation is repeated so often that in the final analysis becomes tiring; it leads one to believe that the sole purpose of papal authority is to counterbalance that of the bishops.

The primacy of Peter is an inestimable gift made to the Church and it must not be reduced to a yoke imposed by brute force. Papal authority must not be used to stifle that of bishops but rather to protect, insure and sustain it. At Vatican II we conciliar Fathers had a great responsibility, not to exaggerate Vatican I but to complete it and to rectify the practical errors it made. Just like in a family, for example, the father's authority confirms and sustains the mother's authority but does not in any way lessen it, so too is the authority of the pope and the bishops. My judgement is that, by issuing *Lumen Gentium* without having revised it to take these vital matters into full consideration, the bishops at Vatican II only partially succeeded. To continue to illustrate using the figure given by the late Patriarch Maximos IV, I would venture to say that though the Catholic Church may no longer appear as a dwarf with an immense head and a tiny body, it still appears to be somewhat deficient or retarded for it does not yet appear to be completely normal.

The interdependence of the head of the college of bishops and the college itself is not only in keeping with the truth but necessary for any profitable dialogue with Orthodoxy, as we have repeated so many times before. The fact that the pope cannot substitute his power for that of the bishops in their own dioceses was clearly declared in a letter of the German bishops to Bismarck in 1875 - a letter that was even solemnly approved by Pius IX, the "Pope of Infallibility." That document could have been inserted into the text of *Lumen Gentium* as I suggested in one of my speeches[1] to the Council Fathers but the plea went unheeded. Nevertheless, though we may be disappointed, let us not become discouraged but let us henceforth follow in this matter of papal vs. episcopal authority the admonition that we "Be sober and watch"[2] And let us keep before us the logic that tells us to attribute all authority to Christ, for is it not from Him that the pope as well as the bishops, obtain all their powers and their priesthood itself?

Moreover, the authors of *Lumen Gentium*, still obsessed with the Roman primacy, seem to have forgotten an essential point, namely the doctrine of Christ the priest and the doctrine of the sacraments instituted by Him. By neglecting the Eucharist they forgot that *it* is the bond of unity inside each Church and within the universal Church.

Catholic theologians often speak of the exercise of episcopal and collegial powers, so long as it is dependent upon the Roman primacy. Is there not another truth to be affirmed and underlined still more, one that could have received more mention in the official documents of the Second Vatican Council? I am referring to the idea that the authority of the Roman Pontiff is not absolute, isolated and independent of the existence of the College of Bishops. The authority of the Roman Pontiff and the bishops can be no more than the authority of Peter and the power he exercised over his college of bishops (the apostles). Now, this type of mutual interdependence is not only a wonderful thing to behold but it also appears absolutely necessary for meaningful dialogue with the Orthodox.

According to Roman tradition, a man is not directly elected to be universal pontiff (although the world press would have us believe otherwise) but *he is elected to head the Diocese of Rome*, which was the final and permanent See of Peter; at the moment of his election this bishop of Rome automatically becomes the Pope of Rome and is then heir to the powers of Peter. Elected to the See of Peter, he succeeds Peter in his primacy, as is acknowledged by both

East and West. Can we forget, for example, the affirmations of the Eastern prelates at the early Ecumenical Councils: "Peter has spoken through Leo" or "Peter has spoken, using the mouth of Pope Agatho" of Rome. And this is why the electors of the Roman Pontiff (the Cardinals, in modern times), regardless of their home dioceses or countries, hold title to church buildings either in the city of Rome itself or in its environs. We are thankful to Pope Paul VI who, following in the footsteps of his immediate predecessor of holy memory, John XXIII, solemnly declared in September of 1963, that the Diocese of Rome was truly his See and his own responsibility. "The College of Cardinals", Paul said, "has willed to elect me to the Catholic Episcopal See of Rome and, *as a consequence of it*,[3] to the Sovereign Pontificate of the universal Church." Just a couple decades or so ago this undeniable truth would never have been admitted so openly, consequently, for a very long time it has been blurred in the minds of the Catholic faithful but today, due to the fact that Christ has inspired recent popes to visit the people in their immediate care, these popes - no longer as "the prisoners of the Vatican" - have taken to the streets to visit homes, schools, churches, prisons, hospitals, and other public institutions, yes, even the slums so that they may visit their children of Rome. The popes have a duty to peoples everywhere, but particularly to those in the Diocese of Rome. It is good to see them now beginning to take this responsibility more seriously.

My thoughts about bishops' conferences that were taken into consideration at the Council (and some of them were incorporated into the final decrees of that body) can be summed up in the four following points, some of which are ecumenically important:

First: The relationship of the Roman Church to Eastern Orthodoxy has grown out of ten centuries of union - the millennium that comprised the formative years of all Christianity - during which the Latin Church not only *acknowledged* the collegial and synodal form of government as used then and now in the East, but also *lived* according to this pattern, together with those traditional and Apostolic Eastern Churches.

In addition to the great ecumenical councils which brought together under one roof the episcopacy of the East and West under the unchallenged presidency of the Bishop of Rome, the Roman Church also exchanged synodal letters with the traditional and Apostolic Churches of the East - letters dealing with problems which concerned both the local Churches and the Universal Church.[4]

In our day, when the Catholic Church is trying to become more accessible to full and visible communion with Eastern Orthodoxy and is preparing for ecumenical dialogue, the only type of church government the West can use *even within itself* is synodal government, i.e. government by *genuine* Bishops' Conferences with *real* power. To speak of conferences which would be purely consultative organs would forestall the possibility of dialogue.

Secondly: episcopal synods or conferences in the Catholic Churches of the East have been deprived of all real power, which has been transferred into the hands of the Roman Curia, especially the Congregation for the Eastern Churches. To convince oneself of this, one need do nothing but consult the new Code of Canon Law for Eastern Catholics.[5] What this congregation actually does is to assume the role of a pseudo-patriarchate.

To take Eastern Catholic patriarchs, who by right are the presiding officers of their Synods, and make them secondary and minority members of a congregation with authority to deal with the affairs of their own patriarchates - as was done a few years ago by Roman Church officials - is actually a condemnation of collegiality in the Eastern form, namely the synodal form of government under the chairmanship of the patriarch.

What should now be put in place of this congregation is a body whose members would be delegates of the episcopal synods or the plenary conferences of each of the Catholic Eastern Churches.

Third: Bishops are the pastors both of Catholic action and the whole apostolate of the laity, and they are the ones who bear the primary responsibility for it. Now this apostolate is no longer limited to the boundaries of definite parishes or dioceses. It is organized on a worldwide scale. Only the collective power of the episcopacy will make it possible for them to carry on their pastoral action on the level of national or universal bodies of the lay apostolate, which should be under the control and direction of the bishops.

Fourth: At the Second Vatican Council some bishops spoke, without any real or objective foundation in fact, in opposition to collegiality and bishops' conferences with juridical power. Their opinions were based on the fear of a dangerous nationalism.

We have now arrived at a moment in history when nationalism, at least if it is not a narrowly centralized nationalism, is no longer a danger to the universal good, but instead a way of enriching the whole of human society.

Actually, as the young nations progress and gain their freedom we see that the international bodies in which these peoples participate on an equal basis become more vital and important than ever before, and Christian bishops, priests and people should not be any less charitable and open to them than are statesmen.

In conclusion, let us recall a quotation from a pope who believed about papal authority as do many Eastern Catholics and was the true pastor of his people. He was also a wonderful man, and we may say in the language of today's youth, one of the "beautiful people", and is known to so many of us as Good Pope John. By his own simplicity, sincere dedication, humility and especially by his warm love, he affirmed that even today the presence of Christ permeates every cubic inch of the world when he admitted: "I have loved every person I have ever met."

Notes

1. October 17, 1963.

2. Cf. 1 Peter 5:8.

3. i.e. The office of Bishop of Rome secondarily carries with it primacy in all the Churches.

4. These synodal letters were not directives but what we might today call dialogues, exchanges witnessing to the faith of individual local Churches and bishops. [F.S.]

5. Here again Archbishop Zoghby is referring to *Cleri Sanctitati*, published under Pius XII. Its Canon 195 reserved to this congregation "all matters of whatsoever kind which regard either the faithful or the discipline of the Rites of the East", granting it "full and exclusive jurisdiction" over the territories of the Eastern Churches. Other canons affirmed the competence of additional Curial congregations in certain matters.

The Codes of Canon Law published for both the Eastern and the Western Catholic Churches after Vatican II were meant to contain only a minimum of directives. Accordingly the jurisdiction of Curial congregations is not mentioned in either one. However the Apostolic Constitution on the Roman Curia, *Pastor Bonus*, published in 1988, which sets forth the competencies of these bodies is often included as an Appendix in editions of the Western Canon Law.

Articles 56-61 of this constitution, which set forth the competency of the Congregation for the Eastern Churches, are comparable to the canons from *Cleri Sanctitati* cited above. The principal canons are as follows:

"Art. 56. Whatever pertains to the Eastern Catholic Churches - whether persons or things - falls under the competency of this Congregation.

"Art. 58 #1 The competency of this Congregation extends to all those matters pertaining to the Eastern Churches which must be referred to the Apostolic [i.e. Roman] See: matters pertaining to the structure and ordering of the Churches, the exercise of the teaching, sanctifying and governing ministry and the states, rights and obligations of persons, as well as any other matters covered in Arts. 31 and 32 on the quinquennial *ad limina* visits."

The reader is left to decide whether there is any real difference between the two [FS].

Fourteen - The Melkite Patriarchate and the Catholic Church

In a discourse delivered at the closing Eucharistic Liturgy of the 1958 Synod of Melkite Bishops, Patriarch Maximos IV said: "The chief concern of the Christian assembly demands that we affirm the eminent position that the apostolic Patriarchs of the East should occupy in the undivided Church - a position due them by right."

These words, together with the spirit ruling over the synod, removed all possibility of reducing the big problem posed by "De Personis"[1] to the stature of merely a local or a community affair. The entire Eastern Catholic hierarchy was especially interested in this Synod, held at Cairo, and saw in it a reaction on the part of Oriental Catholics, showing that they are in favor of preserving and even extending the patriarchal institution. Of all Eastern Catholic bodies, the Melkite Greek Catholic Patriarchate was the first to react to the abominable "De Personis."

Does the Melkite Patriarchate think that its dignity has been more affected by this code than that of the other Catholic patriarchates of the East? Does it claim to have *exclusive* rights upon which "De Personis" might have infringed?

By no means! All the other Eastern Catholic patriarchates are legitimate. They, too, have a right to the same honors and respect in regard to their legal situation. Are they not, too, in the bosom of the Catholic Church?

But if the Greek Catholic Patriarchate felt more quickly and vividly the humiliation inflicted upon the patriarchal institution by this code, it is because our patriarchate is aware that the future of Catholicity and the chances of the success of ecumenism are linked, in a very special way, to the position and dignity reserved to the Melkite Greek Catholic Patriarchate in the Catholic Church.

To understand this, one must realize the exceptional importance of the Melkite Patriarchate from the ecumenical point of view. We will stress here only the representative aspect of this patriarchate.

It is an incontestable fact that the Catholic Churches of the East, once constituted, can have no better destination than to serve as a link between Catholicism and Orthodoxy. They will be able to exercise this role only to the degree that the situation accorded them by the Catholic Church is able to reassure their Orthodox brethren of the nature or the lot awaiting them in case of union.

Just who, then, are those who make up the quarter-billion Orthodox Christians? If we set aside the 12 million Copts and Ethiopians, the three to four million Armenians, the million Syrians and Assyrians, all the others, or more than nine-tenths of all Oriental Christians, belong to the Byzantine rite.

Who in the midst of the Catholic Communion is the chief representative of all these Byzantine Orthodox living in Greece, Eastern Europe, the Near East, the two Americas and, in smaller numbers, elsewhere? None other than the Melkite Greek Catholic Patriarch of Antioch. He is the only one predetermined, both by vocation and by the nature of things, to be the liaison agent between the Catholic Church and the overwhelming majority of the world's Eastern Christians. The eyes of these 250 million Orthodox Christians are now upon the Greek Catholic Patriarch, not in order to judge *him* but to scrutinize the Church of Rome and to see what position it accords him and his people in the Catholic Church. They surmise that they will be heir to the same honors and respect once they come into union with the Roman Catholic Church. An Orthodox prelate once said: "The esteem which Rome has, or does not have, for the Apostolic East will be shown to us by the way it treats the Melkite Catholic Patriarch."

Although we rejoice in - and, indeed, had been the driving force in arranging - the January 1964 meeting of Pope Paul VI and the Ecumenical Patriarch Athenagoras I of Constantinople, as well as their subsequent encounters in Rome and in Constantinople, we state unequivocally that if the Melkite Greek Catholic Patriarch of Antioch does not receive "permission" to exercise the full powers he already possesses, the good-will gestures of past decade or so - visits, returning precious relics, receiving Orthodox delegations, exchanging gifts, etc. - all these gestures of the Roman Pontiff will be worth nothing! If Rome fails to support the Melkite patriarchate, as the popes have promised on numerous occasions in the past, no sensible Orthodox could ever contemplate a union of East and West.[2]

We can state the same thing about the role of other Catholic patriarchs in regard to their Orthodox counterparts and even, jointly with the Greeks, in regard to the whole Orthodox East. To understand the reaction of the Melkite Greek Catholic Patriarchate which is both geared and attuned to its outstanding representative and unitive role, it suffices to simply recognize the numerical, territorial and geographical importance of Churches employing the Byzantine rite in Eastern Christendom. Those who assisted at the Byzantine Divine Liturgy celebrated in July, 1958 at the Vatican Pavilion of the Brussels World's Fair were able to see a vivid illustration of what we have stated above. The same Liturgy, at the same altar, was celebrated at the same time in the same rite by four Melkite Greek Catholic bishops, a Russian Greek Catholic bishop, the Hellenic Greek Catholic bishop of Athens and the Ruthenian Greek Catholic bishop of Pittsburgh, assisted by several priests. The same Eucharistic Liturgy was offered by the hierarchs in Greek, in Arabic and in Slavonic.

The Benedictine monks of the Monastery of the Annunciation in Chevetogne, Belgium, organized the ceremony, and the Slavic choir of Utrecht chanted the service. If there were in Brussels that day clergymen from Bulgaria, Rumania, Slovakia, Georgia or even others of the Byzantine rite, they, too, would have been able to concelebrate this Liturgy while using liturgical books in their own language.

Only the Churches of the Byzantine rite can witness to such universalism and act naturally and normally on the ecumenical plane in this degree of responsibility. The other Oriental rites are usually ethnic and the practice of their rite carried out by a specific group or nationality confined to a limited territory. In other words, they are not supra-national, as is the Byzantine Church. The Catholic Patriarchs of these other rites, in virtue of the fact that they are patriarchs, can be eminent and play a role of the first order, but only within the limits of their own territory.

The "new" title, i.e. the cardinalate (which is quite personal and entirely foreign to patriarchal functions), permits to the patriarchs who accepted it the power to exercise duties which have no relation to those of their patriarchate and which change nothing in their patriarchal, pastoral and residential competencies. Yet, insofar as patriarchs are concerned, the father-patriarch of the Greek Catholics remains, as Archbishop Peter Medawar has said: "the most eminent representative in Catholicism of the living, Eastern, Apostolic Christianity which leavens the human dough of over 250 million souls." This is why we have a keen sensibility and this is the reason for the spontaneous and prompt reaction of the Greek-Catholic Patriarchate in the face of the problems which a codification of Eastern Catholic Canon Law that misunderstands the twenty century-old traditions of the Christian East poses for the conscience of the Eastern Catholic.

I should not wish to insist, on the other hand, on the historical fact that the Greek Catholic Patriarch represents the most authentic and apostolic Christianity in the Eastern Catholic Churches[3] and is, therefore, the legitimate surrogate of the Greek Patriarchs of the East.

Nevertheless, there is no doubt - and this must be repeated - that all the present Catholic patriarchs are completely legitimate and that, for the very good of Catholicity, the Holy See of Rome must act toward all the Eastern Catholic patriarchs in such a way that they can enjoy the traditional prestige, honors and prerogatives which are able to put the Orthodox patriarchs more at ease. The Greek Catholic Patriarch of Antioch must have in the Catholic Church the prestige and honors which the Orthodoc Patriarchs of the Byzantine rite enjoy today. This prestige and these honors, which are much more than merely ceremonial ones, should belong likewise to the Coptic Catholic Patriarch in relation to his Church; to the Armenian Catholic Patriarch in relation to the Armenian Catholics, etc. In other words, we state that the Catholic Eastern Patriarchs should fully enjoy all the powers in regard to their flocks that the Orthodox Patriarchs exercise among their people.

In this area no rivalry is possible among the Eastern Catholic Patriarchs. As the powers of one Patriarch are bolstered, the other Eastern Catholic Patriarchs likewise receive more prestige and power in their own spheres. The only thing that we can state without hurting anyone is that the Greek Catholic Patriarch, since he is, at present, the only representative of the Byzantine world on the patriarchal and apostolic level; this Patriarch occupies by this very fact an eminently important place in Catholicism. This in no way proves that he has a merit superior to that of the other Patriarchs, but it is a *de facto* situation independent of his own worth, independent of his will and of his own personal character traits.

Notes

1. "De Personis" is one of the five title of the Motu Proprio, *Cleri Sanctitati*, written by the Roman Curia, for Eastern rite Catholics and published in 1957. Work on this code was suspended before Vatican II and work on a new Eastern Code begun in 1974. This version was promulgated by the Roman Pontiff in 1990.

2. At one time, the late Patriarch Maximos IV, having become disgusted with Rome, referred to it as: "our holy and 'beloved' step-mother, the Church of Rome."

3. The Greek Orthodox Church is, in fact, the only apostolic Church in addition to Rome, which does not owe its canonical existence to the rejection of an ecumenical council.

Fifteen - A More Democratic Church

The Eastern Churches have always been accustomed to governing themselves without any habitual outside interference. From Christian antiquity these Churches (whether Catholic, Orthodox, Assyrian, Coptic, Armenian or whatever) have been governed by their patriarchal Synods. This is the concept we presented to the participating Fathers of the Second Vatican Council as the authentic, traditional and regular form of government to which the Latin Church should return. We say "return" because the Latin Church had this type of episcopal collegiality in the first centuries but lost it when the papacy began to nibble away at its bishops' powers.[1]

Though Vatican II was over years ago, we united Easterners find ourselves exactly where we were before the Council began. We are still governed by what is in effect a *super*-patriarchate called "the Congregation for the Eastern Churches." All through the conciliar texts we find ourselves being led back, by sly maneuvering and skillful plays on words, to that *Eastern pseudo*-canon law created and unjustly imposed upon us by that same Curial Congregation. And that very same Roman congregation continues to make itself the sole judge of many things in our Churches including the election of our bishops. Also, it denies to our own Greek-Melkite Patriarch and his Synod complete jurisdiction over the emigrant faithful who today constitute the majority of the whole Melkite population. It merely superimposes its veto on any decision emanating from our patriarchal Synod and our will it renders null and void. In fact, nothing important can be decided by us without the agreement of this Curial Congregation!

Moreover, today the very existence of the patriarchal system of rule is being placed on trial. Wishing to honor the Eastern Catholic Patriarchs, the Romans have made them *ex officio* members of the Congregation for the Eastern Churches, dropping them into that body which has never had as much as one Eastern member. This is the Congregation

153

that *runs* the Eastern Churches and only now has it allowed any Easterners even to penetrate its ranks! Since our Patriarchs are now full-fledged members of this Curial dicastery we are expected to be grateful. Yet it takes no genius to uncover the real truth and to see that the vast majority of its members are foreigners - strangers to all that we hold dear - and are from the Latin Church! When this Congregation holds a plenary session to decide a matter pertaining exclusively to one or another Eastern Catholic Patriarchate, it acts as though it were the legally constituted patriarchal Synod, and that the Patriarch responsible for this Patriarchate did not exist. Certainly, the respective Eastern Patriarch is now permitted to cast his ballot as a member of the Eastern Congregation but this is of little avail. What value is his solitary vote against those of some thirty or forty Latin prelates?

I have always wondered why there even *is* a Congregation for the Eastern Churches and, beginning with my very first speech at the Second Vatican Council, I have demanded that it be abolished! This being impossible, I have asked that it be reduced to the level of a non-decision-making secretariat for the *service* of the Catholic Eastern Churches. Such an act would change its complexion from one of despotic domination to that of Christian *diakonia* or useful service.

Now, this Congregation has only been strengthened since the Council terminated. While other Curial bodies have lost some of their powers the Eastern Congregation has actually gained power and still has a tight grip over our Eastern Churches. Its Cardinal-Secretary, whom we admire in all other respects, has been given both the title and the powers of Cardinal-Prefect.[2]

The Western members of this tribunal are several times more numerous than the Catholic Patriarchs and run the risk of soon becoming equal to the number of all Eastern Catholic bishops combined! Recently they have increased their own number by seven eminent Cardinals. One cannot help but see in this a mark of the great esteem the Roman See has for our Churches but can one keep himself from seeing this as a manifestation of the custodial power this Congregation exercises over these Churches and their Pastors? Can we not help but feel literally *invaded* and *deluged*?

Why must so many high ranking personages of the Latin world - members of all races and cultures except our own - be alerted, readied and mobilized, so to speak, to look after our Churches as if we were absentees or minors?

Have we Eastern Catholics exhibited symptoms of dissolution or death in order to require the need of such crushing reinforcements? Did our activity at the Second Vatican Council reveal to the world that episcopate is deficient, retarded, or immature? Are our Churches less Christian than so many Latin Churches of the West, or threatened with disappearing for lack of apostles? Is it that our people are less believing, less pious, less moral than the average Western flock? And our priests, *all* our priests, those of the East and those of the emigration - are they not by the grace of God manning their posts with unshakeable faithfulness? Are they not, like their Orthodox brother-priests, true to their holy vocation while their Western brother-priests are running off for reasons that we prefer not to judge?

This being the case, we do not understand why a Congregation for the Eastern Churches with its numerous and illustrious Latin Cardinals, Latin bishops and Roman prelates must come along to double for our episcopate and to practically substitute itself for us. Why should it continue, in this, the age of democracy, to perform activities that are our own and to impose on the Eastern Catholic Churches a solicitude which we find exaggerated and sometimes even suffocating?

A Suffocating Solicitude

Surely we want to be helped. Who can survive alone in this world? But an aid so massive, exercised by such an omnipotent organization holding powers parallel to and even surpassing those our Synods once had, this aid is not really aid at all. We call it exactly what it is: guardianship, substitution, the usurpation of power, and *unlawful seizure*!

You will have to excuse us, the legitimate pastors of our Churches, for resenting this "invasion" and for finding it inopportune. From before the time of Christ our countries, especially those of the Middle East, have lived under foreign occupation. Without doubt there has been some benefit derived from some of those who were our masters but, having reached a certain degree of maturity we have begun to suffer from it. Consequently, since we wished to regain our self-dignity and independence our countries had no other alternative than to re-win their independence through bloody battles and overburdening sacrifices. Today, the wealthy, prosperous and powerful Western "master" is becoming for us more and more the "brother", the "friend".

You need not be astonished to learn that our Churches, which certainly have no need to envy the Churches of the West, still suffer from a feeling of being occupied or under mandate. Whether we wish it or not, the Congregation for the Eastern Churches with its powerful financial, administrative and human apparatus reminds us of the "Colonial Office" and does not respond to our aspirations or to the wishes, much less to the explicit will of Vatican II which only recalls the constant tradition of the Eastern Christian Churches when it says: "The Patriarchs, together with their Synods, constitute the *superior* authority for all the affairs of the Patriarchate."[3]

We are sometimes tempted to think that by freeing ourselves materially and financially we will be able to achieve a greater administrative independence. This is possible in fact, but we refuse to believe that the dignity and autonomy of a Church must depend solely upon the material means it has at its disposal. Those present at the central see of Catholicity, indeed of Christendom, and who are by this fact deputed to transmit the offerings of the faithful from all over the world to the poor Churches have, like us, the honor of being poor despite the outward appearances of prosperity, and they benefit as much as we do from the charity of the Catholic world. Poverty is not a disgrace in the Church of Christ! The charity of him who gives and of him who transmits the gift takes nothing away from the dignity and pride of him who receives.

The creation of Latin Episcopal Conferences, we thought, would allow us to rehabilitate our own patriarchal Synod, for this is our traditional episcopal conference. But such was not the case. Exactly like the Latin Episcopal Conferences, our Synods can decide nothing definitive. Everything we try to accomplish is subject to revision and approbation, so much so that we rightfully wonder if the patriarchal Synod and the Episcopal Conference are not essentially, and after all is said and done, merely consultative bodies or study clubs.

The Synod of Bishops itself, created in the name of the episcopal collegiality advocated by Vatican II at our instigation is, unfortunately, nothing more than a consultative organ. The members of this Synod know this very well; they have officially been reminded of this more than once.

We are, therefore, since Vatican II, in the presence of a type of collegiality not at all collegial, for bishops, and together with them the entire Church, are reduced to the role of consultors. Though the Council and the first meetings of the Synod received widespread publicity and though the consensus was that the Church's government would now be radically altered, diocesan bishops are still being dictated to by the Roman Curia. Indeed, the very lot of the universal Church is still contingent upon the Roman Curial dicasteries under the vigilant and moderating eye of the Pope.

Now the true collegiality, sanctioned in the East by twenty centuries of Christianity, is not and cannot be this "collegiality of consultation," but is one of *government*. Even the multiplicity of nationalities in the bosom of the Roman Curia does not make it a universal and legitimate. The solicitude of the bishops in relation to the Church, local as well as universal, is of divine right and therefore inalienable. As to the authority of the Curia which (supposedly) works in the name of the Pope through bishops who have received no delegation from the universal episcopate, it can in no way take the place of the authority of this episcopate.

This concept of authority in the Church is not in conformity with the spirit of Vatican II and can do nothing but harm to even the Latin episcopate. It goes without saying that it will meet with the strongest resistance from the Eastern Churches which, from the periods before, during and after the Great Schism, always ruled themselves by means of their Synods.

We Uniates can continue to maintain cordial relations with the Orthodox Churches but we are foolish and absolutely forbidden to speak to them of *authentic* Christian unity as long as a genuinely collegial form of government has not replaced the purely consultative one in the Catholic Church. However, we are obligated to admit that even the new consultative Church in the West is an improvement over the restrictions placed on bishops and their dioceses by the First Vatican Council.

The decrees of Vatican Council II, although still insufficient for the normal expansion of episcopal collegiality, could still serve as a basis for a more effective participation of the episcopate in governing the Church. But most we await the Catholic Church's next worldwide Council to effectively move from the consultative Church to the collegial Church? It appears so. But when that comes about, and only then, will the Catholic Church have eliminated the age-old virus of division and schism, and ecumenism will then be able to pass from the stage of fraternal charity, friendly discussion and *feigned* dialogue to that of *real* dialogue.

Notes

1.   Our brethren of the Western Churches have adequately expressed their reactions to a public statement on Collegiality issued by Cardinal Leo Joseph Suenens of Brussels, Belgium and originally published in *Informations Catholiques Internationales*. Since we feel the Eastern position to be more reasonable than the Latin stance on the many points raised by the Cardinal and those Western Christians who expressed their views, we felt it fitting to set forth this Eastern position.

2. When Pope Benedict XV set up this Curial Congregation in 1917 he retained the title of Prefect (President) of this body for himself and for the Popes alone so that the Popes could restrain the Congregation should it ever be necessary. Now that Pope Paul VI has relinquished these powers to the Curia, can this not be taken as an indication that the Papacy is no longer concerned with our welfare?

3. *Decree on the Eastern Catholic Churches*, 9. The first part of this section bears quoting as well: "In keeping with the most ancient tradition of the Church, the Patriarchs of the

Eastern Churches are to be accorded exceptional respect, since each presides over his patriarchate as father and head.

"This sacred Synod, therefore, decrees that their rights and priveleges should be re-established in accord with the ancient traditions of each Church and the decrees of the ecumenical Synods.

"The rights and priveleges in question are those which flourished when East and West were in union, though they should be somewhat adapted to modern conditions."

Part VI - Aspects of the Church's Ministry

Sixteen - The Indissolubility of Marriage

The problem which probably causes more anguish to young married people than birth control is that of the innocent spouse in the prime of life (usually the young lady, so we shall use the feminine form throughout this chapter to denote the wronged spouse) who is deserted by her partner and contracts a new union. The innocent party goes to her parish priest or bishop for a solution but hears: "I can do nothing for you. Pray and resign yourself to living alone for the rest of your life because you cannot marry again and expect to remain in the good graces of the Church."

Such an unrealistic response is an insult to the young person's inherent dignity! Furthermore, it presupposes an heroic virtue, a rare faith and an exceptional temperament. This almost abnormal way of life is not for everyone. After all, the young person was married in the first place because she didn't feel called to perpetual continence. Now she is being cornered into contracting a new and illegitimate union *outside* the Church so as to avoid physical and emotional pressure. This good and normal Catholic now "officially" becomes a renegade and is even tortured by her own conscience. Only one course of action is left open: either become an exceptional soul overnight or perish!

Nothing but common sense tells us that perpetual continence is not the answer for the majority of Christians in such a predicament. In other words, we Church officials know that we are leaving these young and innocent victims without an answer. We ask them to depend upon that faith which works miracles, but we forget such faith is not given to everyone. Many of us, even we who are priests and bishops, still have a long struggle and a great amount of prayer ahead of us before we will even be able to approach it, let alone attain it!

The question presented us today by these disturbed people is, therefore, the following: "Does the Church have the right to tell an innocent member of the laity, whatever the nature of the problem disturbing him: 'Solve it yourself!

I have no solution for your case,' or indeed can the Church provide in this case an exceptional solution which she knows to be suited only for a tiny minority?"

The Church has certainly received sufficient authority from Christ, its founder, to offer all its children the means of salvation proportionate to their strength. Heroism, the state of perfection - these have never been imposed by Christ under pain of eternal perdition. "If you wish to be perfect," Christ says, but only "if you *wish* ..."

The Church, therefore, *has* sufficient authority to protect the innocent party against the consequences of the other partner's wrongdoing. It does not seem normal that perpetual continence, which belongs to the state of perfection alone, can be imposed upon the innocent spouse as an obligation or a punishment simply because the *other* spouse has proven to be false! The Eastern Churches have always known that they possessed the authority to help the innocent victim and, what is more, they have always made use of it.

The marriage bond has certainly been rendered indissoluble by the positive law of Christ. Yet, as the Gospel of St. Matthew points out: "except in circumstances of adultery." (Cf. Matt. 5:32; 9:6) It is the duty of the Church to make sense of this parenthetical clause. If the Church of Rome has interpreted it in a restrictive sense, this is not true in the Christian East where the Church has interpreted it, from the very first centuries of its existence, in *favor* of possible remarriage for the innocent spouse.

It is true that the Council of Trent, in it's twenty-fourth session (canon 7 of *De Matrimonio*) sanctioned the restrictive Roman interpretation, but it is well known that the final formula adopted by Trent for this canon had been purposely altered so as not to exclude the Eastern Christian tradition. This tradition followed (and *still* follows) a practice contrary to that of the Church of Rome. History gives credit for this act to the representatives from the area of Venice[1] who were well acquainted with the Greek tradition, which was founded upon the interpretation of the Greek Fathers and even of some Western Fathers, such as St. Ambrose of Milan.

We know how the Eastern Fathers tried to discourage widows and widowers from contracting second marriages, following in this the counsel of the Apostle Paul; but they never intended to deprive the innocent spouse, who had been unjustly abandoned, of the right to remarry. This tradition, preserved in and exercised by the East, was in no way dissolved in the six centuries of union. There is no reason why it could not be brought back into use today and adopted by Western Catholics. The progress of patristic studies has, in effect, put in bold relief the doctrines of the Eastern Fathers who were no less competent moralists and exegetes than the Western Fathers.

Pastoral solicitude for the wronged is suggested in another way by Western canonists. By means of a subtle casuistry, which sometimes borders upon acrobatics, they have devoted themselves with diligent application to uncovering every impediment capable of vitiating the marriage bond. This is done because of their pastoral concern. Sometimes, for example, it happens that somebody suddenly discovers an impediment of affinity after ten or twenty years of marriage (one which was unsuspected all the while!) and now this impediment is permitted to afford a complete resolution of the "problem" as if by magic! Though canon lawyers find this state of affairs both natural and normal, those of us who are pastors have come to realize that our people are very often confused and scandalized by this.

It is not the tradition of the Eastern Fathers, as outlined above, more suitable than the impediments to marriage in extending Divine Mercy toward some Christian spouses?[2] Undoubtedly, inconsiderate action cannot be tolerated here either; abuses are always possible. But, the abuse of authority does not destroy authority.

During this age of ecumenism and dialogue, can the Catholic Church recognize this longstanding tradition of the Eastern Churches? Or, what is more important to it: Can its theologians apply themselves to the study of this problem and provide a remedy for the anguish of the innocent party, permanently abandoned by his or her spouse, and to deliver this person from a danger constituting a grave menace to the soul?

My statements above are of a strictly pastoral nature. My aim is to help the Western Catholic Church discover a solution for the problem faced by so many young marrieds who are doomed to a single life of loneliness should they decide to separate. As it is now, through no fault of their own, they are forced to endure continence as a matter of obligation.

In addition, I have clearly affirmed the immutable principle of the permanency of the married state. In doing this, I have purposely avoided using the word "divorce" because the Catholic use of this word clearly denotes an infraction of the unchangeable principal of the indissolubility of marriage.

This indissolubility is so deeply imbedded in the traditions of both East and West, Orthodox as well as Catholic, that it can never be questioned. In effect, the Orthodox tradition itself has always held marriage indissoluble as the union of Christ and His Spouse, the Church, a union which remains the *type exemplaire* of the monogamous sacramental marriage of Christians. In Orthodox theology, divorce is nothing but a dispensation allowed the innocent party in certain, well-defined instances and from motives of purely pastoral concern, in virtue of what Orthodox theology calls the "principle of economy," which means "dispensation" or, more accurately, "condescension." This dispensation does not exclude or set aside the *principle* of indissolubility. This principle is even used in much the same way as the dispensations of a valid, consummated marriage are allowed by the Western Catholic Church through the Petrine Privilege. We are not speaking here of abuses; they are always possible, but they do not change the theological reality.

Therefore, it is this "dispensation" on behalf of the innocent spouse that I suggest be employed by the Catholic Church of the Western tradition. When I referred to the traditional Eastern interpretation of Matthew 5 and 19, I saw the eventual possibility of additional reasons for dispensations to supplement those already admitted by Western Catholics, such as fornication and the abandonment of one spouse by the other, so as to keep away the peril of damnation which menaces the innocent spouse. Such a dispensation would not cast any doubt upon the indissolubility of the marriage bond any more than do the other dispensations.

Such a proposal is not fruitless, despite what certain militant Roman canonists contend, because it rests upon the *indisputable* authority of the blessed Fathers and Doctors of the Eastern Churches - these same saints who are annually commemorated in the Roman liturgical calendar - who cannot be accused of having given up truth while interpreting the Lord's words, or of interpreting the Lord's words to suit their personal ambitions.

It is the perspective of the universal fidelity of the East, as well as of the West, that the Roman Church has *never* contested the legitimacy of the Eastern ruling favorable to the remarriage of the innocent marital partner, either after the separation of the two great Christian halves of the Church, or during their long centuries of unity.

To anyone who has observed the Eastern Catholic communities in union with Rome, it goes without saying that in these days - and it grieves me to admit it - almost all of the Eastern Catholic Churches follow contemporary Latin-Roman discipline and practices with regard to remarriage.

As for the Eastern way of viewing divorce and remarriage, objective evidence proves that the Fathers and Doctors of the East who developed the basis tenets of all Christian doctrine could not have been influenced by politics or any other aspect of Byzantine civil or legal tradition in interpreting Christ's words in Matthew, chapters 5 and 19 as they did. To assume this would be to forget what the universal Church owes to their knowledge and holiness.

The Justinian Code which was promulgated toward the end of the sixth century adopted the Eastern discipline on marriage. But it could scarcely have influenced Origen, St. John Chrysostom, St. Basil[3], St. Epiphanius[4], and others who lived some 350 years before this Code was ever conceived, as some Latin canonists believe. The Justinian Code merely reflected the doctrine and practices of the Eastern Churches.

As we have seen, long before the schism with Rome, Eastern Christianity adopted the more lenient interpretation of the law (favoring the innocent party) and also put it into practice. And yet *the Easterners were never condemned for this* - not during the first thousand years when they were in full and visible communion with the Roman See; not by the

Ecumenical Councils over which presided representatives of the Bishop of Rome and were attended by both Eastern and Western bishops; and not by any other high authorities in the undivided Church. These facts alone should be enough to prove that the Roman Church never contested the legitimacy of the Eastern discipline in this matter.

The Church of the East has always followed this tradition of tolerance of divorce and has remained faithful to it. The West maintained it for many hundreds of years with the *positive approval* of many of its bishops, popes, and councils, and in fact never attempted to condemn it in the East, even after the cessation of its practice in the West.

In conclusion, we reiterate that this is an exegetical, canonical and pastoral problem which cannot be ignored. As for the opportunity of permitting a new reason (or reasons) for dispensation analogous to those already introduced in the Roman Church by reason of the Petrine Privilege, this decision remains in the hands of the Church.

Notes

1. There is still a somewhat large and visible Orthodox population in Venice and vicinity.

2. Father David Kirk, a Melkite Greek Catholic priest (founder of Emmaus House in Harlem, New York City) has recently said: "The tradition of Eastern Christianity is essentially one of compassion. People must be given a second chance. The absolute value of the human person must be underlined.
"Just as the monk can abandon his state in the name of his person, so the same freedom exists [in the Eastern Churches] for a married person. We are not free if we can only say yes at one moment and cannot say no at another moment." (Cf. Rev. David Kirk, "An Eastern Catholic Understanding of Sexuality" in *U.S.Catholic-Jubilee*, March, 1970, pp. 39-42.)

3. St. Basil, in whose immediate family were several saints, was Archbishop of Caesarea in Cappadocia during the fourth century. He said: "I am not sure that a woman who

lives with a man who has been abandoned by his wife could be called adulterous."

4. St. Epiphanius, Archbishop of Constantia on Cyprus during the fourth century, wrote: "Divine Law does not condemn a man who has been abandoned by his wife, nor a woman who has been abandoned by her husband, for remarrying."

See also the following:

"Better to break a marriage than be damned." from *Homily on 1 Corinthians* by St. John Chrysostom (Migne: P.G. 61,155)

"He who cannot keep continence after the death of his first wife for a valid motive, as fornication, adultery, or another misdeed, if he takes another wife, or if the wife [in similar circumstances] takes another husband, the Divine Logos does not condemn him or exclude him from the Church..." from: *Against Heresies* By St. Epiphanius of Cyprus (Migne: P.G. 41, 1024)

For a further explanation of conditions that are tantamount to death so far as the marriage bond is concerned, see *Marriage: an Orthodox Perspective*, by John Meyendorff (Crestwood, N.Y. St. Vladimir Seminary Press, 1970)

Seventeen - The Concept of "Mission" in Eastern Theology

The reader may perhaps wonder what an Eastern bishop can tell him about the missions when the Churches of the East, due to certain historical circumstances and turmoils, have been obliged to suspend most of their missionary activity. However, down through the centuries the Eastern Churches have been very mission minded and they possess a rich and fertile mission mystique of which most people are greatly unaware.

While respecting the intense and admirable missionary activity of the Latin Church, I dare to hope that the Churches of the East will be able to one day resume their own missionary endeavors, for the *whole* Church is essentially missionary. Furthermore, I believe that the modern Church should find its inspiration to promote and support missions and the sense of "mission" not only in the Latin tradition but also in the rich traditions of the Christian East.

Today, the thinking of much of the Church seems more preoccupied with aiding the existing Western missionary activities than with deepening the sense of "mission". The missionary mystique of the Eastern Fathers could perhaps help us in working out a more complete mission theology. The blessed Fathers of Eastern Christianity , whose patrimony we Eastern Catholics preserve and utilize, had different ideas about the Mission of Christ and of the Church but they all boil down to these three:

First, since the early Christian centuries, the Eastern Fathers have considered the mission of Christ in the world as a Theophany (i.e. an Epiphany), or a bursting forth of the divine light into the world of creation. The mission of the Church consists in perpetuating this Epiphany of the Lord and thus preparing the coming of the Kingdom.

The second idea most dear to the Fathers of the East is this. The redemptive mission of Christ and of the Church is exercised in the presence of a humanity already made fertile by the divine seed, the "seeds of the Word" (*spermata tou Logou* in Greek), according to the expression of Saints Justin and Clement, as well as of Origen. The Gospel message, arriving in a land not yet evangelized, does not cast the seed of God's word into souls totally foreign to the Word of God but rather into souls long prepared by the Holy Spirit. Since the very first moment of existence each of these souls receives the creative "Seed of the Word", the divine seed which then awaits the dew of the new morn before it can increase and bear fruit. This progressive preparation of the world for the coming of the Savior has been conceived by the early Fathers as a "divine pedagogy" in which St. Irenaeus and St. Gregory Nazianzen among others, see and admire the providential plan of God: the plan to redeem humanity - a plan that begins for each man at the first moment of his earthly existence.

The Eastern patristic concept of mission has two advantages. First of all, it does not isolate the redeeming Word from the creating Word; redeemed humanity from created humanity. The Epiphany mission is nothing else than the flowing into the world of the divine light communicated to each human being along with life itself!

And just as the Word, in communicating life, has placed into each man the "Seed of the Word", so too the Incarnate Word in redeeming man has communicated to him the fullness of life. Thus, light in the beginning, and the bursting forth of light at the Incarnation; the seed of the Word at creation and the fullness of the Word by the redemption: "Of His fullness we have all received, grace for grace."(John 1: 16).

The mission of the Church is to faithfully follow in the footsteps of the Baptist, who bore witness to the "Light which enlightens every man coming into this world."(John 1: 9) But the mission of the Church does not cease there. Besides transmitting to men the fullness of life, it sustains them in Divine Grace. By thus linking the mission of the Incarnate Word with that of the Creating Word, the Eastern Fathers affirmed the universal character of the mission of the Church.

The second advantage of this patristic conception of mission lies in the fact that it invites the missionary Church to respect this "Seed of the Word" infused into each human creature. This direct action of God in humanity is what the Fathers of the East refer to as "the divine pedagogy."

The Church must begin by discovering the divine Seed in the peoples it evangelizes, and the natural riches which are the fruit of this Seed. The evangelized peoples themselves must not simply receive the Gospel message from the Church; they themselves must, moreover, enrich the Church universal by bringing with them their own assets, for these things are the fruit of this Seed of the Word which they received from God in the beginning and which they cultivated during many centuries under the direct influence of the Holy Spirit.

Since the Word-Redeemer is also the Word-Creator of all mankind, He belongs equally to everyone and He must be at home everywhere - everywhere among His own. Thus, the missionary Church must not superimpose on the people it evangelizes a ready-made Christ from one particular people, culture, or civilization. Peoples who receive Jesus Christ must be able to express Him, to "reincarnate" Him so to speak, to their own image and likeness so that He may be all for all. The Church is catholic, i.e. universal, to the degree that it is capable of recognizing the unadorned Christ (Whom it has originally given to the nations) in the transformed Christ Whom it receives back from them.

In our age when new nations are becoming legitimately proud of bringing their own cultural and spiritual patrimony to humanity and to the Church, it is important that we continue to respect this traditional mystique of missionary activity and to encourage it.

The third fundamental idea we wish to consider is that mission is not the only an Epiphany of the Lord or the only germination of the Word; there is yet another aspect of missionary activity dear to the heart of the Eastern Fathers. In Eastern Christendom, "Mission" is an "Easter", "a paschal outpouring". The sacramental sign of this outpouring, perpetuated until the coming of the Lord, is the Eucharist.

"This cup," Jesus said to His apostles, "is going to be shed for you and for many."(Luke 22:20) Thus it is around the Eucharist that the Church must seal the new covenant between God and men. It is through the Eucharist that the Church implants itself in a nation. So too, the steps by which non-believers are introduced into the Church are those of their participation in the Eucharistic service: the Liturgy of the Catechumens prepares them for Baptism, and Baptism introduces them into the Liturgy of the Faithful, also rightfully called the Liturgy of the Eucharist.

When speaking of the Kingdom of God, did not our Lord remind his listeners more than once of the parable of the feast to which the householder invited not only his friends and fellow citizens who do not come but also all those who want to come?

The mission of the Church, whatever else it may happen to be, consists above all in raising up the table of the Eucharistic sacrifice, in preparing men to participate in it and in calling them to gather around the Lamb. The altar thus becomes the place for the assembling of the People of God and for the establishing of the Church in the new territory.

The Eucharistic presence of the Incarnate Word is, furthermore, the first gift that the Church presents to the people it comes to evangelize. The communion of love, which unites all those who participate in the Eucharistic meal to the resurrected Christ, is both the beginning and the conclusion of the Mission of the Church; a Church awaiting the coming of the Lord. This is the paschal outpouring perpetuated in the Church by the Eucharist. This is dramatically emphasized in the East, for the celebration of the Eucharist is accompanied each Sunday by the Office of the Resurrection. The life of the Church is thus a perpetual Easter and its presence in the world is a liturgy wherein the new covenant between God and man is sealed by the blood of the Savior.

We Christians of the Eastern Churches would be happy to share our experiences and our heritage of "mission" with all in the great Christian family but particularly with our Latin brethren. With that in mind we invite all to come and see what we have, for we believe that the Eastern Christian missionary mystique will enable both East and West to work together in the future in this great work of bringing all non-Christians to the new life of Christ in His Church.

Eighteen - Servant of the Poor

The Church is the servant of all mankind. She must also be the servant of the poor in various ways in addition to giving them the Gospel message for their salvation and the sacraments to nourish their souls. Both of these are tangible proof of Christ's love for and presence among mortals. It is our duty to serve and to offer salvation to all mankind but in so doing we must follow Christ who began his public ministry with works of mercy - curing the sick, feeding the poor, and consoling the afflicted. He began by soothing the bodily miseries which bore some resemblance to death (and often, in those days, led to death) announcing by this victory his own triumph over the death of sin as well as the death of the body. Christ's ministry then, was begun by works of mercy that prepared the multitudes to accept his message of salvation.

The Church was instituted to continue Jesus Christ's mission of love and compassion. This is mentioned often in the official documents of the Second Vatican Council. Presenting the Church in this way reminds the world that the Church, as a mother, really cares for her children. Following the example of Christ, she cares for man's temporal and material welfare not to cunningly lead them to the Faith but because she loves them and wants to give them solace. So before saying that the Church's mission is to assure the eternal salvation of men, the Council Fathers presented her to the troubled world as the author of the many works of mercy spread throughout the world, such as hospitals, asylums, leper colonies, schools, etc., which soothe so many peoples' ills and do so much good. This is probably the most effective way to open the hearts of men to goodness. How many priests, brothers and sisters by their apostolate of charity have opened souls to God's message, souls whom the apostolate of the word alone has never been able to affect in the least. And when we go about doing good, let us employ less didactic language - less solemn and more spontaneous - the language of Mother Church who presents herself to her children and those invited to become her children, for we must address ourselves to the hearts as well as to the minds of men.

After having considered Christ's and the Apostles' mission and that of their successors, let us not forget the Church's "authority of service"; for the world accuses us of wanting instead to exercise an "authority of domination". In response to these critics I wish to say that we Christians, and particularly the clergy, are men chosen from among men and as such are full of limitations and weaknesses. Thank God, salvation is not an ecclesiastical endeavor that we impose on the world, nor is paradise a fief belonging exclusively to us and for which we want to conquer men. We ourselves, who must constantly struggle to bring about our own salvation, must let everyone know that we are not seeking to impose a type of "Christian domination" on the world or to offer men *our* salvation but to humbly present the salvation that comes from Christ alone and to utilize the means which He Himself has placed at our disposal to attain that end.

Our Christian witness can extend into today's world only if it is done in simplicity and poverty and is in direct contact with the poor. Today both believers and nonbelievers are gathered together around the poor and the undernourished. It is there especially that we must be present. This presence of the Church to the poor was affirmed in chapter two of the Second Vatican Council's *Decree on the Pastoral Office of Bishops in the Church*. Bishops, priests and laity must now implement it. How? There are so many ways, but let us begin by being present among the poor and frequently visiting our nearby houses of charity. Bishops should rearrange and even remodel their episcopal residences so that their "palaces" can house and shelter a work of charity and truly appear as a house of the poor. We must urgently and immediately make the presence of the Church felt among the poor if we want it to be present in the modern world.

And since today's world seems to acknowledge little authority except for the authority of service, let us avoid the titles and insignia that vividly recall medieval honors and the spirit of domination. Let us also spare the Pope, the first vicar of Christ crucified, the pain of hearing us refer to him as "gloriously reigning". The Popes call themselves servants of the servants of God and wish to be such in fact. When we address him as the "Holy Father", have we need of adding anything else?

The Church of the Poor

If the Second Vatican Council is to be considered a blessing for the Church and for the modern world, it is also to be considered a great blessing for the bishops who participated in it, for this Council led us back to the pure spirit of the Gospel and to the methods used in this apostolate by Jesus Christ Our Lord.

Certain conciliar Fathers emphasized the obligation for bishops to be poor. Others reminded the participating bishops of their duty to promote all that would help the poor. Kindly allow me to add that the bishop must also love the company of the poor and to be seen in their presence, for did not Jesus do exactly that? But I will not stop at the example of Jesus, who preferred the company of the poor to that of the more fortunate, nor at the spiritual advantages the bishop can derive from contact with the poor. I would rather stress the fact that the company of the poor is today for the apostle, bishop, priest or even dedicated laymen the one big opportunity whereby the Christian can show his witness to the world.

The Christian and non-Christian world alike is pooling all its energies to come to the aid of the poor - and who can deny that in the poor all men may be made to see Christ, as did the disciples on the road to Emmaus? With this discovery we may begin to comprehend the mind of God, the God Who today is bringing otherwise hostile men and nations together in a common fight against the poverty suffered by our unfortunate brethren the world over. The great numbers of the poor and their miserable conditions are scandalous to the entire human race but we are happy to see men of good-will have now met where poverty reigns and are attempting to obliterate it. They have adopted service to the poor as a new form of religious practice - often the only form for many of them. The only churchman who interests them and who they sometimes even approach, is the one engaged in this apostolate and who can help them in it by being intermediary between them and the poor, and isn't this the true meaning of the Christian priesthood, whether clerical or lay? However, the laymen still seems better able to accomplish more in this field than the average clergyman. But this, fortunately, is also changing, for the clergy are fast becoming cognizant of their role "to be all things to all men".

The Christian world no longer sees the bishop as a prince of the Church who, to maintain his prestige, lives apart from the people in his so-called episcopal palace. The modern bishop must renounce his isolationism and comforts so as to be present where men gather together. The bishop must be the "president of charity" not only as administrator but in the same manner as Jesus Christ who multiplied the loaves and distributed them with his own hands: "He gave them to the apostles and they distributed them to the crowds." It is in the distribution of loaves that the pastor will meet both the poor who need to be served and those who wish to serve.

Allow me to modestly suggest that just as we who are bishops are sometimes obligated to take part in official receptions, to sit at the tables of the wealthy and to meet important personages, we must be as much as possible present among the poor and the suffering, mingling with them in the orphanages, hospitals, asylums, schools and even leprosaria! Why shouldn't bishops visit these houses of charity more often, sharing bread with the poor and living their life, if only for a few hours? In so doing we bishops would often attract men to ourselves and would be able to hold conversations with them and bring them the light of Christ's Gospel. This living testimony can often have more effect than the pastoral letters and the more "intellectual" works of our episcopal ministry.

Why should we not share our episcopal residences with an apostolate of charity or with a small group of unfortunates, thus transforming the bishop's house into a house of charity where people will come in contact with the presence of Christ through his vicars, the bishops? Did not Pope St. Gregory the Great have twelve poor men at his table each and every day?

In the Eastern Churches it is often the Bishop's or the Patriarch's residence that becomes a home to the community with its doors wide open to the Christian people. It is here that the works of charity are born, organized, nurtured and carried out. With aid and assistance from the faithful it is from here that the whole region receives aid from the Church. Here in the house of the chief pastor these charitable activities have their offices, their meetings and here also, the bishop or his staff receives the poor at all hours of the day and night. It is this bishop or priest who opens his house and his heart to everyone who is truly the father of everyone including the poor.

While I realize that the modern bishop is very busy and has little time for anything except the most important matters, I think that all his activities cannot have the efficacy of this single living testimony to the poor. Bishops can and should delegate many of their time-consuming office chores to priests, deacons, and laypeople; but when it comes to assisting the poor, bishops should not absent themselves from the honor of being first in line to serve them. And even though under a more juridic system of government it is enough for a bishop to be a good administrator in order to be a good bishop, this is no longer the case today. We now live in times when we should emphasize the pastoral form of government; and a good administrator has never been synonymous with a good pastor. As Bishop M. Mercier has put it, "Progressive bishops have gone to the length of electing to live in humble accommodation in poor districts and converting their episcopal palaces into schools. It would be well if their example proved contagious!"